FIT FOR GOD TO WIN AT LIFE

8 Steps To Block Difficult People & Aim For Your Goals

La Vita Weaver

DEDICATION

This book is dedicated to all of the beautiful ladies who pulled on my heart strings to write this message. Your encouragement and support was truly a blessing. This message is also dedicated to everyone who desires to become better, experience healthier relationships and enjoy life to the fullest.

Last, but not least, I thank God. In His divine ingenuity, He allows painful experiences to produce a wonderful change in us to work through us. And absolutely no one can stop His amazing plans for our lives!

TABLE OF CONTENTS

PART ONE:
EIGHT WINNING STEPS

INTRODUCTION
YESTERDAY'S BULLIES,
HATERS TODAY

As an adult, I vividly remember childhood bullies. I was shorter than most kids in my grade. Then I was placed in advanced level classes with many kids who were bused to our neighborhood school. My friends were of diverse nationalities. But some of my class-mates felt I had to choose sides. On the way home, I was regularly taunted and teased by this group of girls. As they walked behind me, they yelled, "Who does she think she is? She's not better than us!"

Over time, the taunts increased and led to bullying. I was short, but I wasn't afraid. I just didn't want to fight. I had a happy, upbeat personality and I wanted everyone to get along. These girls quickly realized that their threats didn't intimidate me or provoke me to anger. So they criticized my physical attributes. They called me all type of "shorty" names and the obvious "four-eyes" because I wore glasses. A biracial girl joined the crowd to avoid being harassed. One day she got in my face and stretched out her pony tail, teasing that her hair was longer. The tallest girl in the crowd threatened to kick my "little butt". She knocked her fist in front of each eye and swung it across her cheek. I assumed it meant she was going to black my eyes and knock me out. These threats must have gone on for months.

Finally, the day my older sister found out she said, "Enough was enough!" That same day, she quickly walked me back towards the crowd. As we approached the group, she grabbed my arm and pulled me in front of the obvious leader. She firmly told me, "If you don't kick her butt, I'm going to kick yours!" I wasn't angry enough to fight, but her words were convincing. I had seen my older sister whip boys in the neighborhood. Plus she fought boys who picked fights with my older brother. Fighting this bully was a better option than facing my sister's proven wrath.

My bully swung and hit me first, but it didn't hurt. Or maybe the adrenaline rush numbed the pain. I quickly realized that her emotional shots were more painful than her physical blow. She caught me off guard once and I was determined not to get hit again. My dad boxed regularly and trained my brothers. So I mimicked their movements. My bully was a lot larger, so I shuffled my feet and danced around her. I kept my guards up to protect my face. When she realized she couldn't touch me again, she swung wildly and was out of control. She tried to grab me several times. But I stayed focused and was quick on my feet and she couldn't touch me again. As I moved around her, she quickly became out of breath. And when I saw the opportunity, I took several good shots and she fell to the ground.

To the spectators' surprise, I won the fight. Quite honestly, I was surprised too. Apparently, watching my dad training my brothers, racing my dog and climbing trees paid off. My athleticism made me a strong fighter. And my childhood bully ran away crying and deeply embarrassed. Bystanders and followers quickly dispersed. When I returned to school, for the first time in months,

4

the teasing and harassment stopped. And the same girls who once taunted me wanted to be my friends.

In retrospect, fighting was not the best solution. But my sister had a revelation at a young age. Once I faced the leader of this group, her followers retreated. Going straight to the source beat the bullying. And when our parents found out, it was definitely squashed. We learned that the fight could have been avoided altogether. When our parents met, my bully's parents were shocked to find out that their "little" girl was a "big" bully at school.

Decades later, bullying still takes place, whether at school, in the home, on the job and every place where people congregate. Some of yesterday's bullies are adult bullies today. Still others developed intimidating personalities based on unpleasant childhood experiences. Then many of yesterday's bullies are haters today, which is another group of difficult people. Bullies and haters are similar, but display some differences. Much can be written to describe these difficult people we encounter, but I want to highlight some basic characteristics.

Bullies don't feel good about themselves. They try to intimate or threaten others based on their title or position. Or they intimidate others based on who they want you to think they are. Likewise, haters don't feel good about themselves. They criticize you or will try to taint your reputation, so you won't feel good enough. A bully's main objective is to make themselves seem bigger than what they really are. Haters try to make themselves look better by pointing out your flaws. These critics want you and others to know that "You aren't all of that!"

Furthermore, bullies are more blatant and disrespectful. Haters are more likely to hide their true feelings, then tear you down privately. Or they make condescending statements and snide remarks. Bullies carefully target a person they think they can intimidate. They also intimidate or coerce their followers. They mistakenly feel that oppressing others will somehow allow them to remain in control. Haters recruit others by causing division and conflict within relationships. Or they are two-faced. They act one way in front of one person, but is actually dishonest. To fit in with a certain group or clique, they talk about the person behind his or her back to impress others. And haters don't criticize everyone. Jealousy and envy rise in their hearts when someone has something they admire or desire.

Most bullies are actually haters, but all haters are not necessarily bullies. But these groups have strong similarities. Both can be masters of manipulation and deception. While wearing masks of public sweethearts, they are private terrors to their targets. Then once they choose a target, they need an audience and supporters. Other critics feed their negative energy or help justify their tainted views and behavior. Both always seem to be involved in gossip, backbiting, conflicts or some other type of "drama".

What I find most interesting is that neither group can handle when someone stands up to them. When confronted, they tend to shift the blame and label the "target" as the problem. And they can show two extremes. They blow up to shut you down or surprisingly, they play a "victim". Sadly, many people have not healed from painful childhood experiences and still practice unhealthy habits. Yes, adults still play childhood games. And the "hater games" lead the pack. Therefore, this group of difficult people is the focus of this message.

At some point in our lives, we all will encounter a hater. Over these many years, I have experienced the "hater games" on numerous occasions and in different environments. But I had to be realistic. Haters will not go away. We live, work, fellowship and socialize with people daily. And as long as there are people, there will always be a critic in the crowd. Someone is always going to talk about you, criticize you, try to taint your reputation or outright lie on you. There will always be someone who will dislike you without a real reason or disrespect you without a cause. And no matter what you do, it will not be good enough.

Your critic could range from a stranger to a family member. He or she could be a jealous acquaintance, an unfair boss or a competitive coworker. And it is quite disappointing, to say the least, when someone you trusted or befriended becomes your worst critic. If you are not careful, the pain of the deceit will drag you into an emotional pit of despair. Then today, many people broadcast the "hate" on social media. The insults and ridicule of someone who "like" you reach a much broader audience which causes intense pain and embarrassment. "Haters" make sure they get their point across to let you and others know how they feel about you. An ultimate goal is to make you look bad in the eyes of others.

So much can be written about this prevalent topic. I'm sure you have your own story. This message highlights just a few of my experiences. And yes, at times I wanted to isolate myself to avoid the extreme disappointment. The cruel battery of the negativity and deceit is emotionally draining. It makes you want to separate yourself from people or put up emotional barriers for protection. Or your initial thought is to retaliate. But when we do this, we allow the "haters" to win. Instead of yielding to the hurt, anger, and frustration, I had to learn how to overcome the treacherous schemes. If we don't, it will become a stronghold in our hearts and will pour toxins in every area of our lives.

Throughout my life, certain people have tried to control me, criticize me or taint my performance or reputation in one way or another. I believe my personality and stature were part of the reason why difficult people felt comfortable attacking me. They didn't treat others the same way in my different environments. Also, I was never part of a particular group or clique. This made me an easy target to be picked out to be picked on. At one time, I thought that changing my personality and facial expressions to appear unapproachable was the answer. People seem to respect, avoid or fear approaching people who display a serious or stern countenance.

People often perceive niceness and meekness as signs of weakness. But the opposite is true. As a young adult, the boxing skills I learned from my dad were displayed during my police academy training. In addition, I was the first female to win the award of outstanding achievement in the physical fitness department. I broke records in running, push-ups, sit ups and strength and agility tests. To arrest violators of the law and protect the community, I learned extensive defensive tactics skills. Then I was assigned to a high-crime district and exposed to life-threatening danger and the dark side of humanity. After this culture-shocking experience, it was impossible to be intimidated by people in normal everyday living. Although I left the police department early on, the rigorous training never left me. It changed my life forever. Matter of fact, the intense physical training was a motivation to pursue a career in the physical fitness industry.

Over these many years, I've come across so many rude and disrespectful people. Considering my background and training, if people could see a glimpse of the images in my mind, they would be horrified. And they would quickly realize it takes an incredible strength beyond my own ability to be kind to difficult people. The only way I can succeed is to seek the One who knows what's best for me. I choose to be nice to them because of *Him.*

God placed in my heart that the answer was not to change who *He* created me to be. I could not allow the haters to win. I had to refuse to allow critics to steal the joy, happiness and peace I found in Him. I had to refuse to retaliate and play this treacherous game. To deal with their blows in a healthy way, I had to get fit for the hater games. One of the most important lessons I learned is that haters will try to taunt you, but they *cannot* touch you. Their insults, criticism, lies and negativity are distractions to try to steal your focus. But they cannot stop the plans God has for your life. When you trust in Him, He will turn it around and use it to catapult you to your destiny.

To defeat this heavy weight, it is critical to put certain practices into place. To win, we cannot live our lives aimlessly or like a boxer who misses punches. We cannot become sidetracked by a hater's shots. Boxers endure extensive physical training to prepare for a fight. Like a champion, we have to keep our eyes focused on the prize and aim straight for our goals. In the beginning, it is painful as we adapt to new emotional and physical challenges. But with consistency and commitment, we become stronger, wiser, more flexible and better than ever. You'll discover a greater purpose beyond the hate to be used by God in ways you never imagined. This is exactly what happened to me.

One of the recent hater games ignited my passion like never before. Instead of remaining discouraged or upset, the emotional energy became fuel to whole-heartedly pursue my passion. I became more inspired to empower and unite women to rise above the hate and be free to live life to the fullest. In this book, I share eight steps to block the painful blows and focus on achieving your goals. In addition to biblical principles, healthy eating and exercise tips are included to shape your total well-being. At the end of each step are activities for individual review or group discussions. The inspirational messages will uplift your heart and the appendices include relevant topics and scriptures to focus and win.

All of us are deeply affected by the hater games in one way or another. At any given time, we are attacked directly or will experience the distress of someone we care about. And regardless of the team you've played on—the "haters" or the "hatees"—you *can* become fit for the hater games. When we discipline our hearts and minds, we can pursue our purpose with great enthusiasm and joy. Then we can reach out and help others rise before the countdown. It's time to knock out what's not right and be fit for God to win at life. Get ready to roll with the punches!

STEP 1

FLEX YOUR
DIVINE IDENTITY

As a child, I was outgoing and friendly and genuinely liked everyone. It was quite discouraging when certain girls disliked me for no apparent reason. They would roll their eyes, gossip and find a reason to criticize something about me. As an adult, I experienced some of these same attitudes from certain women. I strongly believed if they didn't like me, they didn't take the time to get to know me.

For a season in my life, I retreated in a self-made cocoon to avoid the extreme hurt and disappointment. I became very selective when choosing friends and limited my inner circle. Women often assumed that I thought I was better. But it never failed. Whenever I befriended a woman who didn't feel good about herself; betrayal, conflict and other problems followed. So I immediately disassociated myself and avoided women who displayed traits of jealousy and insecurities.

I never thought I was better than anyone. My intention was to avoid the "drama" and "female rivalry". I never used the term, "hater". Then after one particular incident, my daughter, who is part of the younger generation, said, "Mom, you're dealing with the haters of today". Shortly after, it was confirmed. One day one of my clients placed her hand on my shoulder, stared straight into my eyes and said, "La Vita, when I was younger I hated women like you." She revealed during that time she was unhappy with her life and was not comfortable in her own skin. Therefore, she criticized and picked fights with girls who seemed happy or had something she thought she lacked. She concluded, "But that was a long time ago. Today, I thank God that I know who I am. Today I can honestly say that I love you and appreciate you as my sister in Him."

These comments touched my heart. The answer to one of my long-time questions was confirmed. It also confirmed a major step to defeat what I call the "hater games". One of the most important steps to overcome the intense blows is to know who you are. Knowing who you are is important for both parties. Discovering her true identity freed my client from disliking other women. On the other hand, recipients of the "hate" have to know their identity to stand against attacks and win.

A hater's whole intent is to knock you down and to knock you out. They belittle your character, appearance, abilities, performance or accomplishments and even your relationships. These personal and professional attacks hurt the core of your inner being. And it doesn't matter what you do. A hater will find something to criticize about you. For instance, if you lose weight, they say you're too small. If you gain weight, they say you need to lose weight. If you're a good weight or size, they critique your clothes, hair, make-up, and even take it further to judge your body parts. And on the job, they criticize petty things and show obvious favoritism. They do not hold themselves or others accountable to the same standards and focus on knocking you down.

A hater strives to point out "perceived" flaws in different areas of your life. Their critical view can tear down your image and make you doubt your self-worth and value. Therefore, you have to know who you are beyond a shadow of a doubt. If not, their gossip, ridicule, insults, deceit, and lies will poison your spirit and bully your heart. Ultimately, their attacks can drag you into a negative pit of bitterness and despair. Or they cause confusion and conflict that tear existing relationships apart. Even when you don't believe their critical perspective, you feel so badly that your image, character and reputation were tainted in the eyes of others. Some haters are so deceptive that their skewed views influence other people. This makes you want to defend your reputation or prove to others that they were wrong.

If you base your identity on what others think about your appearance, figure, accomplishments, possessions, performance or talents, "haters" *will* win. When you rely on people to validate your self-worth and value, the same people can lift you up and praise you one day and unexpectedly knock you down the next. Plus possessions and accomplishments can be lost, damaged or stolen and physical appearance will fade in time. But absolutely nothing can ever take away who God says you are. Like the best investments, we become better and more valuable in time as we grow in Him.

I once heard, "Who you think you are can be more important than who you are." This makes perfect sense. People react and make decisions based on who they believe they are. We pursue relationships, careers, jobs, friends, and spouses and other life choices based on this concept. When you know that you are a beloved child of God, you don't have to act out of character when faced with a hater's schemes. You are able to face the attacks and maintain your peace with confidence. You can stand firm when you believe in who your heavenly Father says you are.

- *Who you think you are is important for your life's choices.*
- *You will react and make decisions based on who you believe you are.*
- *You can stand firm when you believe in who your heavenly Father says you are.*

If you negatively respond to a hater's attacks, it validates the effectiveness of their blows. It gives your critic the attention he or she desires. They want to know that they hit you where it hurts. But when you define yourself based on God's views about you, you will not be preoccupied with the hater's perspective. You will discover what matters most is how the One who created you sees you. And there is absolutely no one higher than God. There is absolutely no one greater than God. And when you trust God as your Defense, the hater's blows will not accomplish the intended damage.

You cannot allow people's opinions to define who you are. Human beings have limited views and perspectives. People are naturally short-sighted. But God's thoughts and ways are much higher than ours. He looks down the road and sees the bigger picture for our lives. People see where you've been and where you are; God sees where you're going. People see what you've done; God sees how He is going to use it for your good. People see what you are; God sees the wonderful masterpiece you are becoming. People naturally tend to point out your flaws. God sees the best in you, hopes the best for you and plans the best for your life.

Simply put, your identity is based on who God created you to be. Other people's opinions do not dictate your identity. And their skewed views surely do not dictate your destiny. Therefore, focusing on a critic's perspective is a waste of your precious time and energy. Plus you have to refuse to believe the lies. Keep in mind, no matter how you got here, you were not a mistake or an accident. God knew you and called you by name before you were in your mother's womb. He used your parents' genetic make-up to create your personality and characteristics with a specific purpose in mind.

- *God sees the wonderful masterpiece you are becoming.*
- *Other people's views do not dictate your identity or your destiny.*
- *God sees the best in you, hopes the best for you and plans the best for your life.*
- *Focusing on a critic's view is a waste of your precious time and energy.*

We have to be realistic. If not, we will become victims when faced with the deceptions of the hater's tactics. Absolutely no one is perfect. We all have room for growth. And each of us will be a work in progress until the day we die. And no one person knows it all or has all it all. There will always be someone more attractive, younger, shapelier, more talented, gifted and smarter in certain areas. But every child of God is special. Each of us was given something special. Your gift is not my gift, but *you* have a special gift from God. My gift is not your gift, but *I* have a special ability from above. But we have a choice how to use what God has given us.

- *No one is perfect; we all have room for growth.*
- *God gave each of us a gift or special ability from above.*
- *We have a choice how to use what God has given us.*

If you don't know what your gifts are, ask God. He will reveal them to you at the right time. Other people can also help you discover what they are. Your gifts are not meant for you. They are designed to help others. They are often what you find easy to do and enjoy doing. This is why you may not recognize what they are. They tend to be a natural part of who you are. Friends, family members, coworkers and other people are good sources to find out what you do well. Or they can tell you how you best inspire others. And the more you exercise your gifts, the more they develop and mature. Your gifts were designed to help you accomplish what God created you to do.

- *Your gifts were not meant for you, they were designed to help others.*
- *The more you exercise your gifts, the more they develop and mature.*
- *Your gifts were designed to help you accomplish what God created you to do.*

People tend to focus on others when they don't have goals for their own lives. This makes sense. People who do not have a vision, try to pick apart or kill someone else's dreams. Or they spend most of their time making comparisons or critiquing others. Or they search for greatness in all types of places. But when you know who you are, you can tap into the greatness you already have on the inside. And God uses different paths to lead each of us where He wants us to be.

You don't have to tear others down or envy their gifts, talents, accomplishments or appearance. You can focus on moving forward with the vision God placed in your heart. No one can be you like you. So be the best you, you can possibly be. And when you discover the greatness God gave *you*, you can make something great happen.

- *When you know who you are, you can tap into the greatness you have on the inside.*
- *No one can be you like you. Be the best you, you can possibly be.*
- *When you discover the greatness God gave you, you can make something great happen.*

The fierce competition we see today that rips existing relationships apart and prevents others from occurring was never God's desire. This also occurs when people try to do what God created someone else to do. The Bible is clear that *your* gift will make room for *you*. This world is full of a diversity of causes and people. So surely it is big enough for each of us to share our ambitions, gifts and talents somewhere and with someone. We can celebrate each other's successes, knowing that we all are part of God's greater plan to make a difference.

- *The fierce competition that rips relationships apart was never God's intention.*
- *The world is big enough for each of us to share our gifts somewhere and with someone.*
- *We can celebrate each other's successes, knowing that we all are part of God's greater plan to make a difference.*

God needs people in every profession, in every industry and in every environment to touch people everywhere. He wants to use our diverse backgrounds, experiences and personalities to reach everyone. And it is His prerogative how He chooses to use us. So appreciate the gift He placed in you. Then see others as special creations to make a difference too. When we truly accept our identity, we can embrace each other's differences as the beauty of God's creativity. When we unite our gifts, wonderful and unimaginable things will happen throughout this world. And in God's eyes, *you* are the greatest gift. You were made in His magnificent image to reflect a little bit of heaven on earth.

- *Appreciate the gift God placed in you.*
- *See others as special creations to make a difference too.*
- *We were created in God's image to reflect a little bit of heaven on earth.*

Another important aspect of knowing your identity is to recognize the bigger picture for our existence. God didn't create us to stand alone, but to be part of His royal family. Romans 8:15 says, *"But you received the Spirit of adoption by whom we cry out, 'Abba, Father."* In the Roman culture, an adopted person lost all rights of his or her old family life and gained all new rights as a legitimate child of the new family. Today, the meaning of adoption is pretty much the same. During the adoption process, parents make a conscious decision to commit to caring for a child for life by making the child a permanent member of their family. The adopted child acquires all legal rights as an heir of the new family.

The term "adoption" conveys a strong message. This concept is very important to understand our divine identity. All of us have issues, short-comings and circumstances based on our past. And no one has a perfect family or background. But one of a hater's tactics is to use our short-comings, mistakes and past as admonition to attack our self-image and identity. But you have to know that you were specifically chosen as a child of God. And He chose you regardless of your family, background, education, income, neighborhood and upbringing. When you turn to Him, your past, mistakes, short-comings or poor life's choices cannot stop what He has for you. As Creator of the universe, He created you as His precious child solely based on His immeasurable love for you.

- *You were specifically chosen as a child of God.*
- *God chose you regardless of your background, education, income or upbringing.*
- *Your past, mistakes, short-comings or poor life's choices cannot stop what He has for you.*

As the adopted of God, we can put our old lives behind and look forward to our wonderful new beginnings. Then we can hold our heads up high; not in arrogance, but in confidence of being hand-picked and chosen by God. With Him on your side, as mentioned earlier, haters will try to taunt you, but they cannot touch you. The Bible says, "If God is for you, who can be against you?" Clearly, God has no equal and God has no rival. If they give it their best shot, there is no match for our great God. He has the divine ability to turn all of their harm around for your good. Their insults are weapons to try to get you down. In the hands of our awesome God, they become great tools. He uses them to sharpen your focus and give you a brand new perspective about your identity and life's purpose.

- *You can hold your head up high, in confidence of being chosen by God.*
- *Haters will try to taunt you, but they cannot touch you.*
- *In the hands of God, their tactics are tools to sharpen your focus.*

No matter what anyone says about you, as a King's kid, you are highly favored, cherished and unconditionally loved by God. Before you were born, He had a plan to adopt you into His royal family. As an heir of God, you can enjoy the full rights and privileges of being a child of a King. You have to know that you are somebody! You don't need approval or applause from others. You are royalty in your heavenly Father's eyes. And you have the divine privilege of calling the Supreme Ruler and Creator of the universe, your "Father". What an awesome honor!

- *As a King's kid you are highly favored, cherished and unconditionally loved.*
- *You are royalty in your heavenly Father's eyes.*
- *You have the divine privilege of calling the Creator of the universe, your "Father".*

Accepting our divine identity includes connecting to God's vision for our lives. Then we can avoid falling prey to the enemy's lies. When you don't fit into a particular group or clique, haters want you to believe that there is something wrong with you. A hater focuses on insecurities, uncertainties, and other views to make us doubt who God created us to be. Your identity and self-worth are directly connected to your purpose. If you don't know who you are and who you belong to, you will find yourself struggling in life and confused, without clear direction. You ultimately fail to believe that you are good enough and that there is something greater for your life.

- *Accepting our divine identity includes connecting to God's vision for our lives.*
- *Your identity and self-worth are directly connected to your purpose.*

The Bible says that as a man (or woman) thinks in his heart, so is he. For instance, if you believe that you are a failure, you will easily give up and quit when faced with challenges or attacks. If you believe you made too many mistakes, you will be stuck in past regrets and remain stagnant in life. If you feel you are not pretty enough, smart enough or good enough, you can struggle with insecurities, feelings of rejection and become overly sensitive. You will be afraid to pursue better opportunities or these feelings can lead to the hater games, if not dealt with in a healthy manner. In other words, you will live what you believe. But when you believe God promises for your life, you can accomplish things you never imagined.

During a recent experience, if I had not grown more secure in my divine identity; the insults, criticism, lies and deceit would have caused bitterness in my heart. For if we are not careful, the hater games will be a huge distraction in our lives. The blows on our character, appearance, performance, abilities, and even family, cause anger that disrupts our mood, attitude and overall well-being. Therefore we have to change our perspective. You have to know that God's vision for you is far greater than anything you can ever think about or hope for. His dreams for you, are far bigger than the biggest dream you will ever think about. And He loves you beyond measure. If you focus on their actions, the distraction will prevent you from knowing these powerful truths. The distractions will prevent you from moving forward with the greater purpose for your life with enthusiasm and joy.

- *You have to change your perspective to avoid becoming distracted by a hater's blows.*
- *God's vision for you is greater than anything you can ever think about or hope for.*
- *God's dreams for you are bigger than the biggest dream you can ever dream about.*

Knowing who you are frees you from the lies, intimidation, manipulation, and settling for less than God's best. As a child of God, you have to know that you have been freely forgiven, freely loved and created for a wonderful purpose. When you know who you are, you don't have to tear down others or be intimidated or manipulated by critics. When you embrace your divine identity, you can strive for something beyond yourself. And when you know who you belong to, you can trust in *Someone* far greater than yourself.

- *Knowing who you are frees you from settling for less than God's best for your life.*
- *When you know who you are, you can strive for something beyond yourself.*
- *When you know who you belong to, you can trust in Someone greater than yourself.*

Unknowingly, haters help secure your identity and give you an idea about your life's purpose. Obviously, a hater would not notice you, unless they see something special about you or admire something about you. Think about this: why would they feel a need to fault-find if they didn't see something worth tearing down? And how can they decide they don't like you, when they didn't take the time to get to know you? We often get hurt and offended by their critical comments and actions. But when you are picked out to be picked on, God is preparing you for something greater.

- *When you are picked out to be picked on, God is preparing you for something greater.*

Ironically, haters notice God's glow on you. Even if you don't feel it, God knows His plans for your life. That's why when you show up, they show out. The anointing of being chosen by God makes you stand out from the crowd. And His magnificent light in your life, exposes the darkness in their hearts. They try to discourage you to dim your light and to shut you down. When this happens others cannot see God's amazing joy and goodness in your life. It is not just about you. Someone else is relying on you for their breakthrough. So let your light keep shining and trust God. He wants to bring you out and show you off, to give others hope when faced with difficult people. For they are everywhere we go.

- *The glow of being chosen by God makes you stand out from the crowd.*
- *Let your light keep shining so others can see God's joy and goodness in your life.*
- *Someone else is relying on you for their breakthrough.*
- *God will bring you out and show you off to give others hope.*

If we reverse the painful insults and criticism, haters reveal powerful truths about the calling on our lives. This is clearly illustrated in the Bible. When Jesus was baptized, heaven opened and God's Spirit descended on Him like a dove. And a voice came down from heaven and said, *"You are my beloved Son in whom I am well pleased."* God confirmed Jesus' identity. Then He was immediately led into the wilderness to be tempted. The temptations were attacks based on who God called Him to be. The enemy questioned Jesus' identity and tried to distract Him from knowing the purpose for His existence. The devil's opposition was to abort God's plan for His life.

But God had a plan. Jesus' struggles in the wilderness taught Him how to relate to our weaknesses. The temptations confirmed the reason for His existence. He came out of the wilderness fully prepared and anointed to fulfill His God-given purpose with powerful bouts of teaching, preaching, and healings. The temptations also proved His identity. And absolutely nothing or no one could stop Him from pursuing His passion of setting the captives free and giving us a brand new life.

- *Haters reveal powerful truths about the calling on our lives.*

Once you know this truth, the truth will set you free to spread your wings and pursue your destiny. You'll learn that absolutely nothing is impossible to achieve based on your new identity. And yes, we are not perfect; but we serve a perfect God who does not condemn us. His amazing love strengthens us and helps us overcome our weaknesses. Jesus went through it first for us. Now, He patiently cheers us on to overcome oppositions.

- *Once you know the truth, the truth will set you free.*
- *God's amazing love strengthens us and helps us overcome weaknesses.*
- *Jesus patiently cheers us on to overcome oppositions.*

Sadly, haters try to drag you into their identity crisis. The saying that "Misery loves company" exists for a reason. They have not embraced that Christ went through the wilderness to relate to all of their weaknesses and frailties too. They don't realize that when they turn to Him, He will forgive them, strengthen them and give them a brand new life. They don't realize that they too can be set free to be all that He created them to be. Blinded by pain, jealousy, envy and insecurities, they fail to see that they were also created with a special purpose in mind. Therefore, they really need our prayers.

- *Sadly, our critics do not realize that they can be set free too.*
- *They fail to see that they were created for a special purpose too.*

In conclusion, when you embrace your divine identity, you *will* rise above the hate. Plus you have to accept a well-known biblical fact: Criticism, false accusations, insults, offenses and attacks come with the territory of being a child of God. Jesus' critics followed Him daily, waiting for Him to make a mistake. He was completely innocent, yet He was falsely accused, lied on and hated without a cause. And He had no faults. Everything He did was good to change the world and the lives of others.

If it was done to Christ, surely, we will face criticism, hatred and undeserving attacks. But when we place our trust in Him, the opposition will be a blessing at the end. Jesus' critics were used to push Him to His destiny. Likewise, a hater's blows help build our spiritual muscles and strengthen our character for our purpose. When we place our confidence in God, we can flex our divine identity. We can stand strong in the Lord, knowing that our awesome God is greater than the haters. So start your day by repeating God's views about you. Repeat the following:

-I am a child of God and an heir of God
-I am deeply cherished as God's special treasure
-I was created in God's image to share His goodness with others
-I am wonderfully and fearfully made in His sight
-I am not a mistake, I was created for a reason
-God has an amazing purpose and plan for my life
-There is nothing I cannot accomplish with God by my side
-God sees the best in me and hopes the best for my life
-God knows the wonderful masterpiece I am becoming
-God's dream for me is bigger than any dream I can dream for myself
-I am the freely forgiven to live life to the fullest
-I am loved and adored and I was created for so much more
-God thought about me before I was in my mother's womb
-I am part of God's royal family and He knows me by name
-I don't need applause, I am a star in my heavenly Father's eyes
-God will work all things together for my good
-God is my Defense, I put my confidence and trust in Him
-If God is for me, who can be against me?
-I am not a victim, I am victorious in Christ
-I am somebody!
-With *Christ* I *will* win!

Step #1 Activity

I. Change your views about you. Write down thoughts that prevent you from becoming all that God created you to be. Replace them with God's views about you according to His Word. See the examples below:

<u>*Your Views*</u>

1. I feel like a failure
2. My life will never change

3. I made too many mistakes
4. I'm too old to pursue my goals
5. I feel so alone

<u>*God's Truths*</u>

1. It is nothing too hard to accomplish with God by my side.
2. God has an amazing purpose and plan for my life.
3. God works all things together for my good.
4. God will revive my heart and restore my youth as the eagles.
5. God will never leave me or abandon me.

<u>*Your Views*</u>

<u>*God's Truths*</u>

II. Answer the following questions:

1. Name three things you like about yourself.

2. Name two things you want to change.

3. How do your likes and dislikes influence your views about you? About others?

4. Who or what has influenced your views about you the most? Describe how.

5. What critics' actions or words bother or hurt you most?

6. How can you avoid becoming easily offended?

7. Describe what it means to be a child of God?

8. What do you think is more important to God?

9. How does knowing your divine identity help you overcome insults and criticism?

10. How does knowing your divine identity help you fulfill your purpose?

STEP 2

RECOGNIZE
THE REAL WEIGHT

W hen God created mankind, He breathed His Spirit of life into his nostrils and said, "This is very good". As God's magnificent creations we are special in His sight. And every human being was made by God and for God. As we grow into adults, there is a desperate need to reconnect to our Maker. It can be expressed by an insatiable ache in our hearts that longs for the purpose of our existence. Not knowing who God created you to be or why He created you perpetuates a longing or void within to be fulfilled.

This void manifests in our lives in different ways. It is expressed by people searching for love in all of the wrong places, longing to be accepted, trying to please others, or seeking validation from others to feel valuable. This desire to be accepted, to feel special and loved can quickly develop into insecurity or low self-esteem. Insecurity can take root very early in life and grow deep within an adult's heart. For instance, rejection and abandonment early in life leads to feelings of inadequacy. Comparing children's physical appearance, abilities or talents leads to not feeling good enough or they struggle with jealousy or competition as they grow into adults. Even when done unintentionally, making comparisons and pointing out children's differences cause insecurities in their vulnerable hearts.

When insecurity takes root, it leads to a variety of unhealthy emotions and actions. It can cause obsessions with physical appearance, relationships, accomplishments and possessions. Insecurity can cause critiquing, tearing down, belittling and criticizing other people's appearance, accomplishments, abilities and performance. Some insecure women dress seductively to capture men's attention or engage in a lot of sexual activity to validate their self-worth. An insecure woman may lack confidence in her self-value or capabilities; feel inadequate; or lack trust in herself. Insecurity can cause a person to be shy, paranoid, or to withdraw socially. To the contrary one may have compensatory behavior such as aggression, arrogance, or overconfidence. Insecure people can be underachievers who lack confidence in their capabilities or overachievers who struggle with perfectionism.

Ironically, insecurity can be expressed by the desire to feel superior. Superiority seems to be the total opposite of insecurity, but it is really part of the same problem. Insecurity can be revealed by an unhealthy admiration for others or an unhealthy desire of thinking more highly of one's self. In either case, insecurity and superiority stem from the same root issue. Neither is healthy. God didn't intended for human beings to suffer with low self-esteem. He also did not intend for us to esteem ourselves or others higher than we ought to.

We face these profound issues every day. We see how one group believes it is better than another based on race, religion, education, status, income, neighborhood, title or position. The desire to feel valuable or superior is so deeply woven into the fabric of human beings that when the same groups of people have the same characteristics in common, other distinguishing factors are identified. We see how eye color, hair color and texture, facial features, and complexion are compared within the same races. Still some people strive to achieve the perfect body or certain looks to gain attention or to stand apart from others. Then people's skills, talents, and abilities are measured in the same environments. In the workforce we see daily competition, achieving productivity goals and promotions, often at the expense of belittling and tearing down other employees.

These profound issues of the heart transcend beyond different backgrounds. In over twenty five years in ministry, I learned that a person's socioeconomic status, education, neighborhood, religion or country are not the primary factors of determining one's life. It is the condition of the heart. Issues of the heart contribute to the hater games. Players of this game participate in gossiping, backbiting, envy, jealousy, competition and rivalry on the job, within families and even during fellowships, church or other religious environments.

The reality is people try temporary fixes to feed a spiritual and emotional hunger. This inner hunger must be fed and it goes beyond cravings and sensual desires. Some try to fulfill it with success, money, position, power, shopping, materialistic possessions, relationships, sex, drugs, alcohol, and prescription medications. Even when the fleshly desires have been temporarily fulfilled, there is still an aching and need for permanent satisfaction.

Just as the stomach cries out with hunger pangs for physical nourishment, the soul cries out for spiritual nourishment. The soul needs spiritual healing, wholeness, and fulfillment that only comes from God alone. Seeking a relationship with God satisfies this insatiable hunger within. We were created by God and for God. Feeding our inner man connects us to our Creator who reveals our God-given purpose. Without connecting to our Maker and discovering the reason for our existence, this hunger remains. Many people continue on a life-long journey attempting to fulfill this void. This is a major reason why the hater games exist.

Haters don't tear down everyone. The choose who to "hate". Jealousy and envy are culprits when someone seems to have something they desire or admire. It can range from appearance, possessions, achievements, relationships, personality or attention from others. It can be as simple as admiring the confidence someone displays or the way he or she walks or talks. And once a hater has her sights on you, it doesn't matter what you do. You can do a thousand things right; but your condescending critic waits for an opportunity to find something wrong. And although I mention women in this book, hater games are not limited to one particular gender, race, culture or group of people.

Then it especially hurts when you know you have done nothing to deserve someone disliking you, belittling you or tainting your reputation. But when you realize that the person is not the real enemy, you can look beyond the "hate". You learn that people who look for the worst in others, are afraid to look in the mirror and face the worst in themselves. We can overcome the attacks when we change our perspective and see a hater's game for what it really is. The real issue involves the person's insecurity, hurt, pain, disappointment, rejection and feelings of failure. Haters are actually self-traitors. They deceive themselves by focusing on other people's shortcomings. They find it too painful to deal with their own issues. And even if their action is learned behavior, the root issue is the same. The unhealthy behavior began with someone's pain.

One of my older clients, a 91 year old spunky lady, earned her way to the top of the corporate ladder in a male-dominating culture and career. She became successful during a time when women did not have the same opportunities as men. She said the best advice she could give me is, "Don't take it personally". She continued to say that if I really want to be successful and enjoy the rest of my life, I had to learn how to let people's issues roll off of my back. She insisted not to let them get me down. She said I had to make up my mind to be better than the ignorance and rise above it. With this in mind, I had to change my view and see the truth about the haters in my life. If I was going to win this fight, it was critical not to internalize their negative views and words.

Yes, it feels like a personal attack on your character, appearance, performance and so forth. But we have to refuse to take on this heavy weight. If not, it will lead to blockages in our hearts. As hard as it is to believe, *it is not about you.* You are not the real enemy. You are not the real problem. The real fight is their weight within. People can only give you what they have. We cannot expect for people to like us, when they don't like themselves. If it is not you, the next person will come along and face the pain of the hater's blows. A hater's insults, lies, fault-finding and critical attitude are cries of a heavy heart. Seeing someone who they believe has something better is a reminder of what they believe they lack. Therefore, their actions is really a reflection of how they really feel about themselves. Then they fail to accept that tearing down others is only a temporary fix. They feel better for a moment. But it does not resolve their root issues within.

Realistically, we live, work, socialize and fellowship with people who see life through dark colored lenses. In addition, these unhealthy practices become some people's norm. Like any bad habit, they have been doing it for so long that it becomes part of who they are. These managers, leaders, coworkers, family members, friends and acquaintances expect for others to function with their dysfunction. They commonly shift the blame to take the focus off of their issues. They see everyone else as the problem and hold people at standards they cannot keep.

But their issues within cry out loudly. Their attitude, actions and behavior release negative energy and contribute to unhealthy or hostile environments. And they fail to recognize their need for help and healing. They find it easier to focus on other people's imperfections rather than pursuing change. The tension causes people to walk on egg shells, knowing that someone is waiting to point out flaws or shift the blame.

What also makes it difficult for the "target" is when people believe the accusations. Obviously, when someone is always negative and only point out what's wrong, that person is the real problem. Fault-finding is a strong indication of a deeper issue within the accuser. For there are no perfect people. But God wants to heal all of the unresolved issues of a hurting heart. The only way to have a healthy self-esteem and emotions is to connect to our Maker and Creator and secure our identity in Him. Without healing from God, we all are pretty messed up. Then unhappy people tend to drag others into a pit of despair.

Physical pain is a warning that something is wrong in our bodies and needs healing. In the same way, emotional distress is a sign that something in our hearts and lives needs healing. Whether you're the "hater" or the "hatee", don't ignore the pain. But you have to want healing for change. God wants to free those who have caused pain and the recipients of pain. He wants all people healed, healthy, and whole. Without healing, we will have a skewed view of others and have trouble maintaining and developing healthy relationships. And existing relationships either diminish or lead to emotional distress.

Undoubtedly, we all have been hurt. But God wants to guide the hurting through the healing process. He wants us healthy and He wants us to have healthy relationships with one another. God doesn't want us to retaliate against those who have caused us harm. When we recognize that people are not the real enemy, we can look beyond the "hate" and pray for the healing of us all. Pursuing healing helps you break the hate, so the hate won't break you.

A big part of our healing process is forgiving those who have wronged us. If we look over our faults, mistakes and short-comings, we can forgive others knowing that God forgives all of our wrong doings. When we don't forgive, we remain in bondage to the perpetrator. Forgiveness is not so much for the people who caused us harm. Forgiveness sets us free. The person may never change or acknowledge their faults. But when we don't forgive, the unresolved issue of the heart is like spiritual heart disease that blocks the fullness of God's blessings. These blockages prevent God's goodness, kindness, love, patience, gentleness and compassion from freely flowing in our lives. They inadvertently affect our relationships with people in different areas of our lives.

When I realized that "haters" were in every environment, I desperately wanted to know how to handle this heavy weight the right way. And today I am so thankful for the changes that have taken place in my heart. I am not perfect, but I am a whole lot better. I had to learn how to let it roll off by recognizing the real fight. Sometimes I had to physically take a step back; then roll my shoulders back and take a deep breath. Consciously inhaling in and out gave me the time to recognize the real enemy so I could forgive the person and not take it personally. I realized that "haters" are really the "hurting". It is no excuse to hurt others. But the reality is: Hurt people hurt people; intentionally or unintentionally. And people who feel torn down, often tear others down. Generally speaking, destructive words and actions are indicators of a greater battle within.

We all have been deeply hurt and disappointed in life. Everyone has a story. I've haven't met an adult who has not experienced heartache and heartbreak. If not, the only thing they have to do is to keep on living. Childhood pain, family crises, rejection, marriage and relationship issues cause emotional turmoil and baggage. Some people feel like running away or want to shut down and close off from the rest of the world. Painful experiences cause others to put up emotional barriers to avoid getting hurt again. But it is always there. Without healing, it doesn't go away and affects everything about us.

Unfortunate circumstances in life are physically, emotionally and spiritually devastating. But pain is part of our human existence on this earth. No one is exempt. No matter what we go through, God knows exactly how we feel and He really cares. There is nothing too small for God. And there is nothing so big that He cannot see us through it. Pain and heartbreak lead us to the One who cares the most. You don't have to go through it alone. God is always there to help us. Only God knows the depths of what's really in our hearts. He understands how each of us has been deeply wounded and bruised by life's experiences. It is something about the hurting that captivates the attention of God. And He is so close. His love, compassion, goodness and kindness go out to the brokenhearted. God deeply cares and He wants to heal *all* hurting hearts.

Both the "haters" and their targets need healing. God wants all people healthy and whole and He will gladly help us change. Recognizing the need for healing is a critical step to be free from these issues of the heart. Keep in mind, healing from the inside out is a continuous day-by-day process. God will gently guide us through the process. All we have to do is to ask for His help. But God created us to make choices. He gave us a free will. He will not force anything on you. So the question is: Do you want healing? Then believe and have faith in God. Next, are you willing to do what it takes for change?

When I started my journey of total health many years ago, I desperately wanted healing in every area of my life. I was in so much pain. I had nothing to lose, but I literally almost lost my mind. I struggled with binging, depression and emotional eating. I learned my struggle with binging and emotional eating was less about what I was eating. It was about what was eating me. If I wanted change in my life, I had to do something different.

I took a leap of faith and believed God would heal my heart, mind and total well-being. Then I put action into practice to make it happen. Of course I changed my diet and lifestyle. But in addition to exercising and eating healthier, I had to address the emotional weight within that affected my outer world. I started praying again and reading the Bible daily, even if it was one scripture at a time. I fellowshipped with others to learn more about the Word of God and kingdom living. I connected to people moving in the same direction so we could encourage one another. I read about healing in the Bible, but I had to open my heart to receive it.

God's Word inspired my heart and transformed my life. The Word is our Great Physician's instrument for wholeness. As you read the Bible, the words will minister to your heart for healing and strength. The Word of God goes deep down to all of the woven fabrics of our inner beings and reveal what lies deep within. It discerns our innermost thoughts and reveal who we really are. No matter how we appear on the outside and to others, the Word of God has such living power that it skillfully slices the flesh. It reveals what lies deep in the inner layer that others cannot see.

When you read the Word and believe it, absolutely nothing will be impossible to accomplish with God's help. His favor, presence, and healing power will surround you. The Word of God helped me come a long way from where I started. I never imagined that I would be where I am today. It didn't happen overnight. Healing and becoming whole is a process and I've learned to enjoy the journey one day at a time.

During that time, I wrote my faith-based health and fitness book, *Fit For God: The 8-Week Plan That Kicks the Devil OUT* and Invites *Health and Healing IN*. Little did I know that health and healing would be an ongoing journey. *Fit For God* was written over a decade and a half ago, when I was a younger woman in my thirties. However, the sound nutritional information, exercise tips, scriptures, prayer and praise are still relevant today. But I'm not the same. So much more healing has taken place in my heart. Today, I realize that my books, cd's, fitness programs, and other projects are like personal journals of my step-by-step process of wholeness.

Today, I no longer see myself as a victim. I am a victor! I had to stop focusing on others and my outside world. I had to deal with the root of my poor choices—it was all about me. I had to stop the blame game and stop blaming bad relationships or my "haters". I had to face my unhealthy choices and take responsibility for my own actions. And with God's help, I changed. A child is a victim, but an adult can be a participant. Adults have a choice. I refused to get bitter and I chose to become better.

The issue of past regrets once spilled into every area of my life. Eventually, I sunk into a deep state of depression over life's regrets of childhood issues, failed relationships, family concerns, job choices and financial decisions. But thank God for healing my hurting heart. I'm so thankful that God was right there to safely guide me one step at a time. He doesn't reveal everything to us all at once. Only He knows what each of us can bear. He gradually reveals the areas where we need healing until we are completely free. And He knows when we are ready for the next phase of the process.

In addition, my pity party over past regrets had to go. I stopped focusing on the "if I should have", "would have" or "could have" syndrome. Or "Why did that happen to me and my family and kids?" I learned that we can choose to make the best of everyday that we are given. Not only that, there is absolutely nothing we can do to change the past. Like Sodom and Gomorrah, our past has been disengaged in the flames and exists no more. It's over and done.

Let's try to change the past. Think of the incident in the past you want to change. Put it in the forefront of your mind. Look at it. Now change it. Concentrate a little harder. Did it change? Absolutely not! You just wasted precious time and energy trying to change something you can do absolutely nothing about. Your effort could have been used more wisely to make life better today.

Not only did I learn to stop focusing on the past and life's regrets, I am no longer an enabler or a rescuer. God is the only One who has the power to heal hurting hearts and change lives forever. I know my place as a created being. I'm only a messenger and a witness of what

God is able to do because He has done it for me. Then it's up to the individual to want change bad enough to pursue it.

During this process I also had to change my view and see life from a whole new perspective. I learned to see God in everything. And I learned that God is not a big bad disciplinarian waiting to whip us into shape. He created us with a free-will to choose to love Him and serve Him from the heart. And God never allows anything to happen to destroy us. That's why He sent His Son, Jesus Christ, so we can experience an abundant life in heaven and on earth. God wants the best for us and He works all things together for our good. Trials shape and mold our character. Difficult times allow us to experience that there is nothing greater than God's love for us. We see that He cares about everything that concerns us. Then we can share His love and goodness to give others hope during difficulties and hardships of life.

My critics tried to use my past and poor choices to suffocate my heart and immobilize my mind. And they almost pulled me into their dark pit of negativity and regrets for good. But today I know that there is no one or nothing greater than God. With His help, I was able to put my past behind. Today I see my past regrets as opportunities to reach for God's best. My disappointments, pain, and poor choices led me to the One who could heal me and bring me out. Today, I am so thankful for the changes that have taken place in my heart. And I am so thankful that I am no longer in bondage to the heavy emotional weight that almost took me out. God allowed me to see the hater games from a whole different perspective. Now I can wholeheartedly pray for these hurting hearts.

Hebrews 12:1 says, "...*let us lay aside every weight, and the sin which so easily ensnares us, and let us run with endurance the race that is set before us.*." In this passage, our spiritual journey is compared to a runner preparing for a marathon. This race is not a sprint. It requires stamina, commitment and endurance to make it to the finish line. Preparation requires runners stripping off anything that will hold them back. Gossiping, negativity, complaining, criticism, lying, fault-finding, backbiting and any harmful acts against others are heavy weights that hinder our quality of life. Anger, resentment, insecurity, jealousy, envy and any type of ill-feelings toward others are distractions from our goals. And heavy weights do not necessarily have to be sinful acts.

When we recognize the hater's heavy weight and seek healing, we can let go of the emotional weight. God doesn't want anything to slow us down. He wants us spiritually trim to fulfill our purpose with vitality and joy. Are you willing to take a leap of faith and trust God as your Healer? The psalmist said, "O Lord my God, I cried out to You, and You healed me" (Psalm 30:2).

Step #2 *Activity*
Signs of a hurting heart:
The list below is not inclusive. But it contains potential warning signs of a hurting soul and heavy heart. If not dealt with in a healthy manner, these issues can lead to the hater games. Obviously, no one is perfect and we all have room for growth. But the more you check, the greater opportunity you have to seek God for healing and wholeness. And remember health and healing is a process of getting better day by day. Check all that apply:

1. __You have trouble connecting with others.
2. __You have trouble communicating effectively.
3. __You are overly sensitive, defensive or easily offended.
4. __You easily feel rejected, abandoned or unloved.
5. __You have low self-esteem, insecurities or feel inadequate.
6. __You seek approval from others to validate your self-worth.
7. __You are critical, judgmental and point out people's flaws.
8. __You have trouble celebrating other people's successes.

9. __You are preoccupied with looks, accomplishments, or possessions.
10. __You compare your looks, accomplishments and possessions to others.
11. __You complain, gossip, or focus on the negative.
12. __You struggle with envy, jealousy and competition.
13. __You are demanding, manipulating or controlling.
14. __You feel like a failure and struggle with past regrets.
15. __You have trouble forgiving and tend to hold grudges.
16. __You are a perfectionist and things have to be done right.
17. __You are selfish, self-centered and focus on your needs.
18. __You are self-righteous or do not examine your own faults.
19. __People around you feel oppressed, trapped or in bondage.
20. __You do not respect other peoples' opinions, ideas or differences.

Signs of a healing and healthy heart:
The following list contains signs of a healthy heart. Again, health and healing is a process. We get better in time as we seek God for wholeness. You can use this list in a number of way. One way is to mark the opportunities for growth. Another way is to mark the areas where you have grown with a "G". Then identify areas where you need to grow with an "N". Again, this list is not inclusive. Use it as a guide as you seek healing and strive to have healthier relationships. We all have room for continued growth in every area of our lives. This list helps identify some of those areas.

1. ___Your heart is open to freely share God's goodness.
2. ___Your heart is open to love God, to love yourself and to love others.
3. ___You are friendly and open to new relationships.
4. ___Your communication with others has improved (tone, words, expression).

5. ___You see the good in people rather than focus on their faults.
6. ___You don't judge people's outer appearance.
7. ___You have a positive attitude that encourages others.
8. ___You forgive those who cause you harm.
9. ___You are kind, caring and patient with others.
10. ___You encourage others and refuse to tear them down.
11. ___You are able to celebrate other people's successes.
12. ___You are not overly sensitive, defensive or easily offended.
13. ___You focus on nurturing true beauty within the heart.
14. ___Your self-worth is based on your identity as a child of God.
15. ___You put the past behind to enjoy God's newness of life.
16. ___You respect other people's ideas, opinions, and differences.
17. ___You don't compare yourself to others but strive to be your best.
18. ___You make healthier life choices and choose healthy relationships.
19. ___You are not preoccupied with appearance, possessions and accomplishments.
20. ___You connect to positive people moving in the same direction to live better.

Say this prayer:

Dear heavenly Father
Help me to be all that You created me to be. Help me to embrace my true identity as a child of God who has been created for so much more. I believe that You have a purpose and an amazing plan for my life and I am special in Your sight. Now heal my heart God, so I can be all that You created me to be. Help me refuse to tear others down, even when it's done to me. Give me the strength to forgive

others as You have forgiven me. Help me to recognize the value in myself that I may see the value in others as wonderful creations of God. Thank You for loving me, planning the best for me and giving me another chance to be free. Thank You for healing me, as I pray for the healing and wholeness of all hurting hearts. Amen!

STEP 3

LET IT GO
& GROW

Hurt, pain, anger, disappointment, resentment, betrayal, humiliation and embarrassment are some of the many feelings that arise from the hater games. The list goes on and on with the emotional disruptions of the heart. But any emotion that distracts us from living a happy, healthy and fulfilling life is not God's will. He never allows anything to happen to devastate us or destroy us. Trials are designed to help us grow. People often say they want change in different areas of their lives. And we have often heard the long-time saying, "No pain; no gain". But we have a choice. We can allow painful experiences to make us bitter. Or we can choose to learn from them and become better.

For instance, when you start a new exercise program, in the beginning your muscles are sore. The discomfort discourages some people and they quit exercising altogether. But when you hang in there, in time your muscles grow and adapt to the new activity. As you continue to work out, you are able to handle heavier workloads and greater physical challenges. Plus increased lean muscle tissue burns unwanted pounds and helps define and reshape your body faster. On top of that, when people notice the positive changes, you are encouraged to keep working out.

This is what happened during my latest hater's round. It was painful. But the more I hung in there, the better I became. I had to let go of the unhealthy emotions. And it was not easy. It was hard work. I had to make a conscious effort to stop focusing on the negativity. I had to stop replaying it over and over in my mind. I had to stop repeating the insults, which only poured toxins into my own soul. Then I had to stop focusing on the hurt. To get over it, I had to think positive, speak positive and be positive by focusing on God's promises daily. Then I had to choose how to respond to others and the world around me in a healthy way.

Of course, we are emotional beings. Quite honestly, some things won't roll off easily. But if you don't take control of your emotions, your emotions will take control of you. If you don't let it go, a grudge will consume you. And if you don't forgive, you will become bound to an emotional dis-ease that will block God's flow of goodness in your heart. As mentioned earlier, critics will never go away. There will always be somebody somewhere who will talk about you or dislike you without a cause. If you focus on the negativity, it will consume you. The preoccupation makes it hard to concentrate and complete your daily activities. You will be easily irritated and moody, have trouble falling asleep, or toss and turn at night, and then have a hard time waking up to start your day.

Then you feel embarrassed or angry when you think someone is throwing shots at you on social media, talking behind your back, keeping a list of your mistakes or recruiting others to dislike you. Ultimately, a hater's blows will steal your peace, rob your joy and make you paranoid. If reeled in, you will develop a defensive mindset. That is, you'll always be on the alert. This creates anxiety as you anticipate the next insult, criticism or attack. This bullying of the mind is emotionally and physically draining. The worry and frustration places unnecessary stress on your mind and body. Research has linked stress as a major contributing factor to various illnesses and diseases. Hater games can be treacherous. Therefore, they can cause deterioration of your overall quality of life.

Focus on the good for peace of mind

How do we avoid the frustration when negative situations and people are all around us? How do we avoid becoming consumed when they won't go away until the end of time? In the beginning of creation, the world was dark and void and in a chaotic state. God was not consumed or preoccupied with the darkness. He brought something good out of the chaos and created the light. God provides an example of how to handle dark areas in life. Focus on the good. Philippians 4:8 confirms where to place our focus. It says, *"Finally, brethren, whatever things are true, whatever things are noble, whatever things are just, whatever things are pure, whatever things are lovely, whatever things are of good report, if there is any virtue and if there is anything praiseworthy—medicate on these things."*

Complaining, condescending statements, and gossiping are poison to our hearts and minds. God did not create us to handle these unhealthy actions. Therefore, we cannot allow negativity, conflict, condescending statements, gossip and confusion disrupt our mood, attitude and overall wellbeing. The passage above describes how to take action and fix our minds to be free. When we focus on things that are true, honorable, right, pure, lovely, admirable, and excellent and worthy to be praised, we can eliminate the contamination of the hater games. And God's peace will guards our hearts and minds.

God's peace is a great defense when faced with different life's challenges, including difficult people. God's peace is like soldiers protecting our emotions, attitudes and thoughts from outside threats of danger. This peace is far beyond what the human mind can ever possibly understand. It is not self-generated and it is much deeper than positive thinking. This peace is having the inner confidence and assurance that God is in full control. It sooths and comforts our inner spirit to walk victoriously, as we find rest in Him.

God's peace protects our minds and hearts from emotional distractions that keep us bound. So the next time a "hater" or anyone brings you emotional "drama", refuse to get involved. Then fix your mind on the goodness of God. Being consumed by a critic's comments is a huge waste of precious time and energy. God wants us to live in peace and share His light of joy wherever we go. It is impossible to focus on a critic's negativity and give your full attention to the goodness God wants to accomplish in your life. If you have to refuse to take a phone call, do what it takes to protect your mind. If you have to write scriptures on index cards and read them at your desk, do what it takes to stay focused. Or if you have to surround yourself with beautiful images of God's magnificent wonders, do what it takes to keep your mind focus on His greatness. God's peace will be your strength.

In addition to meditating on the goodness of God and His Word; our choice of TV shows, movies, music, books, magazines, internet sites, entertainment, friends, and environments are critical to living a peaceful life. They feed your soul (mind, will, thoughts, and emotions) positively or negatively and will enhance your spiritual growth or turn you away from God. These choices will help you get in good spiritual shape or contribute to unhealthy emotional weight. Total health starts from the inside out. What you put in your body, will determine your thoughts, the words you speak and your actions. In addition, we have to accept the fact that we cannot change people. Our motive for focusing on the position should not be to change others. It should be to become better and make a positive difference right where we are.

Cast your cares on God

Yes, at times, it is difficult to let go because it feels like a personal attack. But "haters" definitely help us recognize our need for growth. Our emotional attachments are what cause us to react. Therefore their tactics show us our sensitivities and what we find offensive. We discover our doubts, uncertainties and insecurities. We learn what makes us angry, irritated, sad and hurt. We learn what we value and where we place our priorities. A hater's attacks test if we place our hope in what people think about us or *our* abilities, accomplishments and reputation. Haters' attacks reveal issues in our hearts that we didn't know exist. We learn if we really place our confidence and trust in God's provisions and promises.

1 Peter 5:6-7 says, *"Therefore humble yourselves under the mighty hand of God, that He may exalt you in due time, casting all your care on Him, for He cares for you"*. Humility doesn't come naturally. When we are wronged or talked about, the first reaction is to defend ourselves. We want to attack back, prove our point, or give someone a piece of our mind. But humbling ourselves under God's hand is when we trust our lives in His care and protection. We don't have to act out of character, prove anything to anyone, walk on eggshells or be intimidated when the Most High God of the universe is our Defense. The Bible says that God's goodness and mercy shall follow you all the days of your life. You don't need to retaliate when God's got your back.

God is truly concerned about everything that concerns you. He sees when someone treats you unjustly or criticizes you to make themselves look better. He sees when they taint your reputation in the eyes of others. He hears every negative comment and every lie. He sees every prejudice and unfair action. God has a reputation as our Creator and Maker. He created us for good works and with a specific purpose in mind. Therefore belittling His children goes against the very nature of our creation. God doesn't want you to take it personally. As parents protect their children, *He* takes it personally. Your critics cannot even hold your past against you. And He says the good work He started in us *He* will complete it.

Therefore, you have to know that God cares how you feel. He cares what happens to you. And He cares when you're hurt, disappointed and made to feel less than what He created you to be. When we become overwhelmed by what others do or say, we may want to retaliate or take actions in our own hands. But the Bible is absolutely clear about revenge. We should put others in God's hands. We should put our reputation in His hands. Put your ego in His care for healing. And trust your career, your future and all of your worries, troubles and struggles in His hands. When we take matters in our own hands, it gets worst. But when we trust the attacks in His care, we see how He turns everything around for our good. Plus one day, every single human being will give an account to God for every negative action and word against others. Everyone will be rewarded accordingly. It may seem like your "hater" has the upper hand today, but God *will* show up strong on your behalf at His appointed time.

In the meantime, it takes humility to recognize that we need God's help. We need His help to focus on the good and not take it personally. Ask for His help. He's so close. He already knows what's going on; He's just waiting for you to talk to Him about it. Then when you're faced with a difficult person, you don't have to respond with a negative reaction. You can cast it on God. "Cast" is an aggressive action word meaning to throw, fling or toss in a forcible manner. So immediately throw all of your concerns, anxieties, worries and stresses to God. Let Him handle them. If you don't, it will take hold of you.

"Cast" is also a term meaning to throw out a lure with a fishing rod. A "hater" throws the bait and you are the big fish they want to catch. They wait for you to react. They wait for you to behave disrespectfully. This shows that you were hit where it hurts. They want to disrupt your mood, attitude and overall wellbeing. Or they need the confusion and distractions to cover their life's disappointments. Refuse to play this treacherous game. If you play a hater, there are no winners. There is only the hurting hurting others; the angry making others angry; and the broken, rejected and bruised pouring toxins of pain in the lives of others. Then there are the miserable who loves the company. If you take the bait, you will get stuck in their hook and have limited mobility. When you refuse to bite, you are free to focus on what really matters to freely pursue God's best for your life.

The power of focusing to succeed

Keep in mind, that a hater's game is only a distraction. You have to guard your heart like a fighter in a boxing ring protects his face, head and body from the blows of the opponent. In this game, the boxing ring is your mind. The hater's blows are only effective if you give them the power. The mind is where the knockout or win takes place. So the real fight is your focus. When you take control of your emotions you can avoid getting sidetracked.

Like a runner aims for the finish line, you cannot allow the burn and the heat distract you. You have to push through the pain to succeed, knowing that it won't last forever. Change will come in time and you will be stronger. But you have a choice. You can waste your time letting the hate take control of you. Or you can let it go, grow and use the emotional energy to bring something good out of it. Choose to focus on what's really important. And use the mental charge to push you closer to your destiny.

Surprisingly, difficult people help discipline our minds. Our reality is our situations or environments will not change immediately. And your reaction will either feed the negative energy or defeat this opponent. But the mind is where the victory takes place. When our minds our free from a hater's blows, their words and actions will no longer get us down or keep us down. Like a boxer disciplines his or her body to prepare for the fight, women especially need to retrain our minds. If not, the hater games will knock us out. As highly emotional beings, women easily become offended, angry, deeply hurt, agitated and irritated. If you fail to deal with these emotions in a healthy manner, you will want to retaliate and play a hater. This will be a huge distraction and you will fail to focus on everything God has for your life.

Our critics teach us how to take our feelings off of our shoulders. They teach us how to refuse to participate in emotional drama. If you made a mistake and was lured in for a moment, turn to God and ask for forgiveness. He will forgive you and He will give you a clean new slate. Then He wants us to humble ourselves and trust that He is fully able to take care of it. God knows how to capture your critic's attention and He knows how to humble them. Don't fight a battle that only God knows how to handle. The same bait they used to try to tear you down, God will use to exalt you. And the more they talk about you, lie on you and attack you, the more God will raise you up for all eyes to see.

Then hate the action, but don't hate the person. Recognize it for what it really is. It is a useless game that hurts those who participate. Don't let the hate break you. Don't retaliate. Rise above the hate. Someone has to be the bigger person. Someone has to be the peacemaker to show that God is real in their lives. Matter of fact, there is always someone watching your reactions. You may be someone's proof that they can survive these attacks with God on their side.

So the next time a hater throws a shot, "Stop!" Don't react. Take a deep breath and let it roll off of your back. Then cast it on God to take care of it. Matter of fact, as a child of God, let it slide off of the oil of His anointing that surrounds you. Then know that God is sharpening skills you will need where He's taking you. Strive to become better every day as you focus on the ideas and dreams God placed in your heart. God will use every single experience to prepare you for the next level.

This reminds me of an experience I had when I attended the police academy many years ago. One of the many lessons I learned is the power of focusing to succeed. I vividly remember our intensive testing, specifically, the push-up test. We had to perform standard push-ups and each one had to have the proper form to count towards the final number. I started out really strong and had reached a number that was high for a woman or a man. Near the end, I was blinded by pouring sweat and the pain of tiring and tightening muscles was so severe that I started shaking. I knew I was done. But before I hit the ground, my defensive tactics trainer kneeled and yelled in my face, "La Vita! That is what your body can do; focus and show me what your mind can do!"

When I heard him call my name and speak with such conviction, something happened to me on the inside. He seemed so confident that I could do so much more. So I thought of a number in my mind and somehow found the strength to focus on that goal. Amazingly, I pushed through the distractions of the sweat and pain and performed thirty-five more push-ups. My final count was well over a hundred and was one of the highest numbers of the entire class. Since that time, this one event has influenced many areas of my life.

I learned as exercise disciplines the body, focusing helps discipline our minds. And the pain is only a distraction. But when we focus on a specific goal, with God's help, we can push beyond the pain to achieve it. And God will use all of our experiences to get us to the next level. He will also put people in our path who will see what He's placed on the inside of us. They will encourage us to push beyond where we are to reach out destiny. If we used this concept to focus on our God-given purpose, powerful things will happen.

Haters help God's children reach our destiny
God knows how to prepare a table before you in the presence of your enemies. Joseph's story in the Bible is an incredible illustration. It reveals how haters' schemes prepared Joseph for his destiny. We see how to overcome the hater games by trusting in someone far greater than the hate. When you get a chance read the entire story in the book of Genesis for yourself.

Joseph was next to the last son of his father's twelves sons and was born in his father's old age. Therefore, Jacob loved Joseph more than his other sons. Plus he made Joseph a special coat which appeared as favoritism to his other children. This special gift added resentment to Joseph's already strained relationship with his brothers. And when his brothers saw that his father loved him more, the Bible says they "hated" him and could not speak peacefully to him. On top of that, Joseph had dreams that he would one day be a ruler. His dreams were not a secret and he shared them with his family. His brothers hated him even more because of his words and his dreams.

Similarly, God can have a calling on our lives that make us stand out from the crowd. Then people tend to envy the dreams, gifts, talents, and our relationships, which result in an unfavorable reactions such as resentment. Sometimes we are so excited or amazed, that we share our gifts, abilities, dreams and accomplishments with others. But if we are not careful, this can appear as being boastful or prideful to others. Then we have to remember that the vision God places in our hearts is for us. Everybody will not be able to receive what God wants to accomplish in your life. Joseph's father had a relationship with God, yet he rebuked his son when he heard his dreams.

When God reveals His vision, we need to first ponder it in our hearts and trust Him to show us when or if we should share it. Even when we have the right attitude and intentions, everyone's heart will not readily receive it. Not only that, some people don't feel good about their own lives. So they clearly do not want to hear good things happening in your life or future. Joseph's brothers were already upset. He was the favorite child and was given a special coat that set him apart from his siblings. They clearly were not interested in hearing about his successful future.

Plus when God shares a dream in our hearts, He doesn't reveal the entire story. If Joseph knew the whole story, his family would have celebrated the dream and would have been thankful. But sharing a dream that he was going to be a ruler over his family in part, added fire to their insult. The dream accurately revealed that God had a special calling on Joseph's life. But Joseph had no idea that it would take many years of growth to fulfill this vision. Nevertheless, his brothers could not see beyond their hate. After Joseph shared his dreams, it was the last straw. Then his brothers plotted to kill him.

One day they found the perfect opportunity to get rid of him. They saw Joseph alone, grabbed him, stripped off his coat of many colors and threw him into a pit, without food or water. Can you imagine hearing their younger brother cry out and yell for help in a deep dark pit? Jealousy, envy and hatred are so deceptive that it burned their conscious. They were able to sit down and eat a meal, while their baby brother cried out for his life.

When jealousy and envy take root in the heart, they can grow into bitterness and hatred. These intense emotions lead to all types of evil thoughts and behavior, such as wanting to cause someone harm, or wanting the person completely out of the picture. This is exactly what happened. After his brothers plotted to get rid of him they said, "Let's see what will become of this dreamer's dreams." They mistakenly thought that getting rid of Joseph would kill his dreams.

One of the older brothers talked the others out of killing Joseph, so they sold him into slavery. When they returned home, they lied to their father and said that a wild beast devoured Joseph. They handed him Joseph's coat that was stained with an animal's blood. Jacob said that he would go down to his grave mourning Joseph's death. He wept and wept and none of his many sons and daughters could comfort him. The brothers somehow thought that their lives would get better without Joseph. But their family life would suffer a great loss, as their father suffered with many years of intense grief and heartache.

What's worst is that the brothers didn't realize that Joseph's dream was a glimpse of their family's blessing. If they would have killed Joseph, they would have died too. God was going to use Joseph to save his entire family and nations of people from starvation when a famine would sweep through the entire land.

But unresolved jealousy and envy burned in their hearts and they could not see beyond the hate. Can you imagine the pain and betrayal Joseph must have felt?

Psalm 105:19-21 says, "*Until the time that his word came to pass, the word of the Lord tested him.*" Every trial that Joseph experienced until the time his dreams came to past was preparation for something greater. What if we changed our view and looked at a hater's game as only a test. What would you do? You would make every effort to past the tests, right?

From the age of seventeen to thirty Joseph was being tested as preparation for his kingdom assignment. A huge part of his test was his *response* during trials. He was thrown into the pit and sold into slavery by his own brothers. He chose to obey God and was falsely accused of a sexual crime, and then he was thrown into prison. Not only did his brothers sell him, but his mother died. Plus he was separated from his father and younger brother whom he deeply loved, for so many years.

After each event, Joseph could have blamed his brothers for selling him into slavery. Or he could have blamed his father for believing the lie that he was dead, instead of looking for him. Or he could have blamed God for allowing the injustice to take place. He became a slave, had the reputation of a sex-offender and then was forgotten about in prison. He should have been furious, right? He should have wanted to retaliate, right? Doing the right thing had seemingly wrong results. But Joseph had the right attitude. His troubles and injustice became opportunities to learn, to grow and to trust God had his best interest in mind.

Throughout his life there was one crisis after another, but God would use each one to train him to run an entire nation. Yes,

Joseph would be trained by his pain. Joseph couldn't know how to be a leader at home. He could not possibly lead an entire nation of people coming directly from the provisions of his father's care. He was next to the youngest child and was obviously his father's favorite. He could have been spoiled and self-centered; and possibly boastful or prideful. Only God knows. Joseph was taken from his earthly father's care to grow stronger in his heavenly Father's hands.

Every trial prepared him for his purpose. But God showed him favor. And because God was with him, whatever he did, the Lord made prosper. In prison, Joseph was shown favor and was assigned to manage the prisoners. Who would have imagined that God would use prison to teach management, economics and people skills? I believe in prison he also learned how to show compassion to those who didn't deserve kindness. His low places gave him a heart to care about the injustice and well-being of the less fortunate. During Joseph's preparation period he had to have met the rejected, the forgotten and the downtrodden. He was in a position to relate to people he may have once thought were beneath him; or he would have never met to learn how to meet their needs.

Like Joseph, our character is connected to our future. The bigger the vision, as with Joseph's dreams, the bigger the tests and the greater the preparation process. God has great plans for our lives and He truly wants to bless us. But He also wants us to grow where we can handle the blessings. We have to be equipped to handle the challenges that come with greater doors of opportunities.

In the meantime, God doesn't want you defeated by the hater games. He wants you to have peace to freely soar to your destiny.

He also wants your character to match where He's taking you. Can you imagine what would have happened if Joseph would have remained stuck in a pity party of despair and anger due to the hateful acts of others? He was able to look beyond the hate and allow God to prepare his heart for something great.

At the time, his brothers didn't realize that God is all about people. God's plan is never about blessing one person. It is solely God's prerogative who He chooses to use. But ultimately, He blesses us to be a blessing, as in Joseph's story. But his "dream killers" allowed their jealousy, envy, and hatred to get in the way. Nevertheless, they could not stop the plans of God.

At the end, what his brothers did to harm Joseph, God turned around for good. God used the lowly places to train Joseph in wisdom, humility, and knowledge to serve in the high places. And in literally one day his whole life changed forever. At God's appointed time, when Joseph's character matched his position of royalty, he was immediately released from prison. That same day his prison clothes were removed. He was clothed in royal garments of fine linen and gold was placed around his neck. Then Pharaoh took off his signet ring and put it on Joseph's hand. This represented Joseph serving in the palace in one of the highest positions in the whole land. Pharaoh was ruler in name only, while Joseph made all of the decisions in the land.

Once reunited with his brothers, they feared Joseph would seek revenge for their evil actions. But Joseph had tremendously grown. He developed the character to let it go. He was able to genuinely forgive, put the past behind, and look beyond the harmful acts. He accepted that God's ways and thoughts are much higher than ours. And the same brothers that threw him into a pit, witnessed his new position of royalty. The same brothers that envied and hated him, had to humbly come to him to save the lives of their entire family. We cannot imagine how they felt when they realized they almost killed the very person chosen to save their lives.

Joseph did not boast in his new position. After years of preparation, his heart was filled with God's love and compassion. He was humbly grateful for all that God had done. The dream had come to past. But this time he boasted in the goodness of God. Instead of showing off what he had, he was able to help those in need. Joseph recognized that God allowed his injustice so his heart could be prepared to save nations of people, including those who caused him the greatest harm.

His brothers' actions could not stop Joseph's dreams from becoming a reality. Years prior, they asked what would become of his dreams. But they learned that no one can stop the plans of God. Matter of fact, they were used to catapult Joseph to his destiny and shape his character for greatness. And once united with his brothers, Joseph left the consequences of their actions in the hands of God. In Genesis 50:19-20 he said to them, *"Do not be afraid, for am I in the place of God? But as for you, you meant evil against me; but God meant it for good, in order to bring it about as it is this day, to save many people alive"*.

Today, people often admire others and seek to envy other people's accomplishments. But they don't know what that person endured to get where they are. Some of the strongest people have gone through some of the toughest trials. A hater's actions cause excruciating pain. But in Chapter One of this message I stated how haters can secure our identity and reveal powerful truths about our life's purpose. When others tear you down, it's a strong indication that God has a plan to raise you up. The more they tear you down, the higher God is going to raise you. Joseph's "haters" specific actions indicated how God would bless his future. God literally turned all of their actions around for good.

For instance, Joseph's brothers threw him into a lowly pit; but he served in a high place in the palace. His brothers stripped off his coat of many colors that was a gift from his father. But he was clothed in royal garments and given gifts of gold. His brothers sold him into slavery. He ruled in one of the highest positons in the whole land. His brothers wanted him dead. He would live and save his entire family and nations of people from starvation during a famine in the land. Then Joseph was a good looking man. He was falsely accused of a sexual crime by a married woman. She was angry that he refused her gestures for sexual relations. But God would remember Joseph's faithfulness. He was blessed with a wonderful wife and family beyond what he ever imagined.

Joseph endured much pain. But God tremendously blessed Him and showed him uncommon favor in the land of his affliction. His character was strengthened by his trials. Then Joseph was able to stand boldly and present the One and only Living God before Pharaoh and an entire heathen nation. This story clearly reveals God's sovereignty. We can let go knowing that God's plans are not dictated by human actions. When others intentionally cause us harm or taint our reputation, God has the divine ingenuity to use all of it to grow our character. So if you want to hold on to something, hold on to God's promises. Hold on to the dreams He placed in your heart. And at the appointed time, God will turn all of the impossibilities into a brand new reality. It will be worth letting go to grow!

Step #3 Activity

1. Describe some of the dreams God placed in your heart.

2. How have sharing them with others affected your life?

3. What are some important life lessons in Joseph's story?

4. How can they relate to situations in your life?

5. What is your initial response or action when someone hurts you?

6. How can painful experiences help you grow?

7. How can you move beyond the hurt, disappointment or anger?

8. What are some areas in your character or life that need growth?

9. What steps can you take to let it go and grow?

10. How can you stay focused and overcome distracting blows?

STEP 4

STRENGTHEN YOUR LOVE WALK

Many women go through the daily motions, but are unable to fulfill their life's purpose with joy. Women smile on the outside, but cry loudly on the inside. Women move forward in life, but have trouble shaking off life's regrets. Women advance in careers, but the pain of the past grips tightly and replays over and over in our minds. Women care for children and families and attempt to help others, while they desperately need healing. Women try to forgive and try to let go, but are haunted by the pain of lies, betrayal, abuse, mistreatment and shame. Many hidden issues of the heart manifest in the inability to appreciate other women. This mindset can inadvertently contribute to the hater games.

In the beginning of creation, God formed man and woman for different tasks. We both were created to bring honor and glory to God. However, one of women's specific privileges is to conceive and bring life into the world. In order to carry life, we are naturally more emotional beings to express a tender deep-seeded love. As nurturers, we have the profound ability to extend the love and compassion to nurse and care for children and to devotedly love our husbands.

Our innate ability to love so deeply is a small glimpse of our Creator's tender side. He created women's hearts like temperature controls to positively influence the atmosphere. We should pour the beauty of His grace at home, on the job, during fellowship, in the community, at the grocery store, the doctor's office, and everywhere we go. We should be the cream in the coffee, the lemon in the tea, the cocoa in the chocolate, the chips in the dip, and the pep in the step.

Unfortunately, our natural affections emotionally backfire at times. This nature is so deeply woven into the fabric of our inner beings that are hearts are easily shattered. Painful blows make our hearts ache and break simultaneously. We expect people to give us what they do not have. We expect people to love us when they don't love themselves. When our expectations are not met, we get easily offended. Or women can throw up emotional walls of protection to avoid further despair.

Emotional barriers make women appear stern or insensitive, which is the opposite of God's design. Deep pain of a wounded heart contributes to the inability to love God's way. With the same intensity we're able to love, is the same intensity we're able to shut down and block God's flow. Without healing, we find ourselves in a pattern of unhealthy thoughts, behavior and relationships.

God understands that women are deeply emotional beings. He understands how we have been affected by our upbringing, relationships, painful experiences and limited understanding. He gave us our innate tender side; but He wants our hearts healed to be used the way He intended. And God is absolutely amazing. His love is so incredible that He loves us understandingly. He knows *all* of our human's frailties, hurt and pain. He sees beyond our faults and weaknesses. His love extends beyond where we've been and beyond where we are. God wants to heal our real dwelling place. Strengthening our love walk will revive our hearts to dance to the rhythm of God's heartbeat.

Genuine love looks out for the best interest of others

"Love" encapsulates the theme of the Bible and the entire gospel message. God Himself describes just how much He really loves us. Our very existence and creation were motivated by His immeasurable love. God loves us unconditionally. There is absolutely nothing we can do to earn His love. And there is nothing we can do to ever lose His love. His love is not selfish or self-centered; it unselfishly reaches out to draw others in. God's immeasurable love extends far beyond human comprehension. This means regardless of where we've been and what we've done, nothing can separate us from the love of God. God's love sees beyond our mistakes and short-comings. And there is no situation dark enough or deep enough that the love of God cannot reach down and snatch us completely out. God's love never fails and it never runs out. And no matter what side of the games you've played on, "haters" or "hatees", God's incredible life-changing love can set you free.

God shows us the pattern of true love. Then He wants us to receive it and freely extend His inexpressible love to others. Genuine love is not the type of love portrayed and romanticized in the movies. And it is not based on physical attraction or lust. This love is not conditional based on our expectations of others. God's love allows spiritual fruits to freely flow in our hearts in a way that we see people from His perspective. Then we can respond to others in a biblical manner. God's love is not based on what we say. The words are meaningless without a sincere heart and sincere action. This type of love is not based on making us happy; seeking to please our own desires; or expecting something in return. True love is a deep, abiding, selfless love that genuinely looks out for the best interest of someone else.

God does not want us to only love those who love us. Evil people love their own. God tells us to love our enemies and those who cause us harm. He wants us to love those who mistreat us, lie on us and speak negatively about us. Yes, He wants us to love our haters. In addition, everyone's personality and behavior will not appeal to our liking. Some people's actions will turn us off and our reactions may seem beyond our control. But God wants us to embrace all people with His love and treat everyone with the same respect we desire.

People who genuinely love are active and steadfast in faith. Hardships, pain, injustice, and disappointments do not stop the flow of love. Real love endures conflicts and challenges and lovingly treats someone else by trusting God. Love refuses to gossip, criticize or cause harm. Love builds others up and refuse to tear someone down. Love thinks the best, hopes the best and sees the best in people; opposed to the worst. Love views others as wonderful creations of God who He can work in and through at His appointed time. Love seeks spiritual growth and maturity while trusting that God is working all things out for good in every situation.

As stated before, we often get hurt by our expectations of others. We expect others to love us when they don't love themselves. We want people to give us what they do not have. But God wants us to love others whether they love us or not. Showing undiscriminating love for our enemies and our loved one and friends distinguishes God's children from others. We should have high standards that separate us from the crowd. As children of God, our actions should reflect His character. God's love reaches out to all people and He wants us to do the same.

Obviously, this love does not come naturally. It goes against our self-centered nature. Genuine love is divine. It comes from God alone. Next, it is a choice. Yes, in the midst of pain, disappointments and betrayal, we need God's help to love. The Bible says that the Holy Spirit pours His love into our hearts. Therefore, it is readily available. When we empty out more of ourselves and release how we want it to be or how we think it ought to be; we can receive more of this divine flow. It can be done when we pray and ask for God's help.

Loving does not mean that we will no longer get hurt. Loving God's way will be painful at times, especially when those we love fail to treat us the same. But God wants us to love in the midst of the hurt. Loving our enemies marks genuine followers of Jesus Christ. Only hearts and minds that have been committed to Him are able to love those who have caused us harm. In this way, we strive to continuously grow and mature in our relationship with God. And those who feel utterly destroyed by a relationship had their hearts in the wrong hands. When God is on the throne of our hearts, He is in the right place to strengthen our love walk and heal our wounded hearts.

In addition, people focus on gifts, talents and accomplishments. But 1 Corinthians, Chapter 13 says without love our gifts are meaningless and useless. Without loving others, gifts are used for self-motivated gain. Therefore, they have no real value to the hearts of God's people. If we want to check our love walk, we should examine our relationships with others, including our enemies. Beware:

There are times when you may not know the real condition of your relationships with others. Many people go along to get along. They find this easier than sharing how they really feel. They would rather please people than risk being rejected. But if someone has to go along to get along, that is not real love. That is a type of emotional bondage. Genuine love allows us to freely embrace each other's differences; even when we have to agree to disagree.

Love is our primary source for life

In Luke 10:27 a lawyer stood up testing Jesus and asked Him, *"Teacher what shall I do to inherit eternal life?"* Jesus answered, *"Do this and you will live"*. He continued to say, *"Love the Lord God with all of your heart, with all of your soul, with all of your strength, and with all of your mind, and your neighbor as yourself"*. According to Jesus' response, there is life in loving God and loving others. You mean to tell me that love brings life? We see this symbolically in Joseph's story. His brothers wanted him dead because of their hatred. With God's love, Joseph's was able to forgive his brothers and literally save their lives.

Today, our "haters" may not physically try to take our lives. But their critical words and behavior can kill our joy, peace, and hope. Love helps us forgive and look beyond their faults. Then we can pray for their broken spirit and ask God to strengthen our hearts. Loving God's way has dual benefits. As the heart pumps vital nutrients and oxygenated blood through our bodies to sustain physical life, God's love sustains our spiritual lives. Every time we choose to love, we experience an amazing flow that strengthens, heals and cleanses our soul. Plus genuine love, especially when wronged, maybe the only proof some people see that God is real. Strengthening our love walk has the divine ability to influence someone's eternal destination.

Ultimately, God's primary attribute is our greatest weapon to overcome difficult battles. Every time we extend love, this life-giving flow strikes against the enemy's plan of destruction. The enemy's grip gets weaker and weaker until the final knockout and God's people are set free. And the more we strengthen our love walk, the more we are able to experience healthier relationships. At times we can love the hate away. Other times, people and our circumstances will not change immediately. But the flow of God's love in our hearts will help us change. That means the things that once got us down won't get us down the same. And the people who once irritated our spirits won't affect us the same. Or if we get down, it is only for a moment, but we won't stay out for the count-down. God's love is our source for an abundant life.

God commands us to love. Jesus sums up and embodies the love of God. And the Holy Spirit pours God's love into our hearts. This love is freely poured from the throne room of heaven and is available to everyone. All we have to do is open our hearts to be a vessel of this divine flow. We often speak of our vision without ac-cepting God's vision for our lives. God's ultimate vision is for His children to be conduits to share His immeasurable love with all people on the earth.

As we grow in our love walk, we can ask God to give us the wisdom to deal with difficult people. But keep in mind that loving God's way does not mean that you accept mistreatment. Expressing the love of God does not mean that we become doormats to be trampled on or punching bags for emotional blows. God's love helps you refuse to retaliate and forgive the person. Then God's love gives you the strength to let go while trusting exclusively in God. And depending on the condition of their hearts, He may lead you to love from afar. Or He may lead you to shake the dust off of your feet and keep it moving. We cannot change people's behavior. But God's love helps us refuse to allow their behavior to control us. God's love teaches us how to protect our hearts and set boundaries to stay healthy and whole.

Our upbringing can influence how we accept the love of God
A harsh reality is that it is hard for some people to love others. One reason we've heard is that you cannot love someone else when you don't love yourself. But when you realize how much you are really loved by God, you can love yourself. With this in mind, Mother's Day is a beautiful celebrative event. Mothers receive accolades, gifts, flowers, cards, and dinner engagements for recognition of our unconditional love for our children. Church pews quickly fill as children and adults join mothers for Sunday Worship services. Mothers are known for our heart-wrenching love for our children and our willingness to sacrifice so much of ourselves to help them anyway we can.

What I find interesting is that the first mention of "love" in the Bible is not a mother's love for her child. It is a father's love for his son (Abraham and Isaac). The second mention of "love" is a husband's love for his wife (Isaac and Rebekah). Not only is this story symbolic of God's love for His Son; it leads me to believe that a father's love prepares children to have healthy relationships with God and with others.

Unfortunately, many people have distorted images of a father or mother based on their upbringing. Or the thought of a "father" or "mother" is painful. This can be based on their disappointment in their parents or the absence of one or both parents. If the image of a parent is distorted in a child's mind, it affects how he or she views God, as they grow into an adult. We all are different, therefore our reactions will be based on our emotional make-ups, personalities and sensitivities.

Colossians 3:21 says, "*Fathers, do not provoke your children, lest they become discouraged.*" God designed the parent-child relationship to prepare children for their relationship with God. Our authority carries over to help children understand God's love and authority. Being a parent is not a license to mistreat children or control children, which will discourage them. Parents are accountable to God to handle children with patience and gentle loving care. God gave parents the assignment and privilege to help them grow into healthy adults that will love and serve God and others.

Parents often carry guilt as children grow into young adults due to regrets of past decisions or mistakes. However, there is absolutely nothing that can be done to change the past. Regardless of our children's ages, today we can plant positive seeds of God's love and goodness into their hearts. Then we can pray that God uproots the unhealthy weeds and trust Him to bring forth a harvest of the healthy seeds at His appointed time.

God is the Creator and Maker of all creation. His love extends far beyond our earthly parents' ability to love us. He is our ultimate Father. He used our parents' genetic make-up to create us. As our heavenly Father, He is loving, kind, gentle, compassionate and comforting. God is never abusive in any way. He corrects us to bring out the best in us. His discipline does not have painful emotional or physical scars. His correction frees us, heals us and delivers us to receive all of His amazing blessings. His love is like a soothing balm to comfort all wounds from our painful life experiences. God never rejects us or condemns us. His love accepts us just as we are, but His loves does not leave us the same. His love uses trials to help us grow and shape our character. His love makes us better so He can trust us with something greater.

What's the condition of your heart?

The physical heart is the major organ for life and affects the health of the whole body. In the same manner, mothers' and wives' hearts affect the relationships and the condition in our homes. Employees' and managers' hearts determine the condition of the work environment. Likewise, pastors' and leaders' hearts influence the condition of the church. Have you been at work or another environment and when a certain person shows up suddenly you feel a thick cloud of tension in the room? Our inner selves (the spiritual heart) determine the health of our environments.

When the physical heart doesn't function well, other bodily functions are affected, which increases the risk of illnesses and diseases. Similarly, gifts, skills and knowledge alone won't get us far if we don't know how to treat others, communicate effectively or nurture healthy relationships. Clearly, people can move up in popularity, position, title or on the corporate ladder. But they will be low on God's spiritual ladder without a healthy heart. What God thinks is more important. He is the only One who can accurately judge our motives. And He sees the true intents of our hearts.

When we look at our environments, we have to ask ourselves: "Do we bring life or death? Are we part of the problem or do we help with the solution? Do we have blockages that hinder a good quality of life? Or are God's fruits freely flowing from our hearts into the atmosphere?" Each of us is a vessel supplying the home, church, workplace, and community with a life source or a dis-ease. What's flowing through your spiritual vessels?

To make it plainer, does the environment improve when you show up? Or to the contrary do you spill the negative effects of criticism, distress, uneasiness, complaining, control, fault-finding, stress or tension in the room. Do your words, attitude, actions, and expressions build others up or discourage others? Do you know if people feel better or worst in your presence? Or have you ever thought about it? Do you even care? God truly cares. And one day every single word and action will be judged by Him.

Ultimately, God wants to liberate all people through the power of His love. Then we will gain the vital nutrients for a healthy inner life. God's healing, peace, joy, hope, goodness, kindness, strength and all spiritual blessings will flow from our hearts to make a difference in the lives of others. And God's love has cleansing properties to remove the toxins of anger, bitterness, resentment and unhealthy thoughts that lead to playing a hater. When we demonstrate this type of love, especially to those who have wronged us, our heavenly Father is well pleased. Walking in love does not mean we will have a perfect life. When we keep our minds on Him, it guarantees perfect peace.

Our sincere act of love provides assurance and proof that a spiritual revival or rebirth has taken place in our lives. Our hearts were created as gifted containers to dispense *God's* sweet fragrances. Like a potter molding clay, His ultimate goal is to return our heart to its original design. And then God can use us as conduits for heaven's flow to touch down and spread throughout the earth. For love is the greatest and most powerful force in the universe. Love is the greatest weapon to defeat all of the hater games. Can you imagine what we could accomplish if we choose to unite and love the hate away? Love will always win because God is love.

Step #4 Activity: Check your love walk
Select one of the ratings below for each category and total your score.

(0) Never
(1) Sometimes
(2) Mostly
(3) Always

1. ___I am patient with others
2. ___I am understanding
3. ___I am kind and respectful
4. ___I rejoice when the truth wins out
5. ___I keep the faith
6. ___I am hopeful
7. ___I look out for the best interest of others
8. ___I hope the best for others
9. ___I endure through every circumstance
10. ___I do good to those who cause me harm
11. ___I pray for my enemies
12. ___I respect people's differences

(0) Disagree
(1) Somewhat Agree
(2) Agree
(3) Strongly Agree

13. ___I never give up
14. ___I am never jealous
15. ___I am never envious
16. ___I am never selfish
17. ___I am never rude
18. ___I am never boastful

19. ___I am never proud
20. ___I refuse to gossip
21. ___I refuse to criticize
22. ___I refuse to condemn or tear others down
23. ___I do not hold grudges
24. ___I do not keep records when I am wronged
25. ___I am never glad about injustice

Total: _____/75 maximum points

Answer the following Questions:

1. What categories have higher ratings?

2. What categories have lower ratings?

3. Can you honestly say that God's love is freely flowing in your heart at all times? Why or why not?

4. Do you demonstrate God's love with everyone in your life? Why or why not?

5. How do you rate your love walk?

6. What does the total score of this activity mean to you?
   One way is to divide the total number of points by the 75
   maximum points
   Example 43 points/75 points maximum = 57.3%

7. Describe what walking in God's love mean to you.

8. How can you strengthen your love walk?

9. What obstacles make is hard to love difficult people?

10. How can you overcome these challenges?

STEP 5

EXERCISE
REAL BEAUTY

A hater's blows really hurt. Our initial reactions are unkind thoughts and the desire to react with unkind words or actions. Then doing the right thing often feels wrong. But the more we practice what's right, the stronger we become in time. In the meantime, we can refuse to retaliate and throw shots to tear others down. You can refuse to lower your standards. How? Like physical exercise improves the overall health of our bodies, exercising real beauty shapes the overall condition of our hearts.

Physically, we are bombarded with images of beauty. When you stand in the grocery store lines you see beautiful images of women on magazine covers. When you drive on the highway there are billboards of alluring women to draw eyes to the advertisement. When you turn on television everything seems to be about the perfect body and sexual appeal. Cars, food and everyday household products are advertised with images of beauty and sex. As we go about our daily chores of life, there is no way to escape the clear message that it is all about the way you look.

Society's preoccupation with outer beauty causes many people to struggle with an obsession with physical appearance. Today, many women look at supermodels, entertainers, singers and actors as role models for feminine beauty. Some feel inadequate when they do not measure up to these standards. But society's views are clearly superficial. The focus on physical beauty is like a quick-fix diet. People want the appearance, without gaining the internal benefits for a better quality of life. Then surprising, many beautiful people who are admired by others struggle with insecurities. Therefore, real beauty is beyond what you see on the outside.

The Bible describes the image of real beauty. 1 Peter 3:3-4 confirms that we should not be consumed with the outside adornment of the body such as the clothes we wear, our hair, make-up, and jewelry. Personal hygiene, proper grooming, neatness, and cleanliness are all necessary. But outer beauty should be kept in its proper perspective. Our primary focus should be to cultivate the gracious inner beauty that is precious in the sight of God.

Outer beauty has its place, but it *will* fade in time. Genuine beauty of a gentle and quiet spirit never fades. It constantly grows and it is enhanced in time. We should focus on developing the inner qualities that reflect a God-centered life. This beauty within has so much more value in our lives. In a culture bombarded with images that emphasize physical perfection, it takes a unique and rare quality to nurture real beauty. And it takes a strong character to withstand society's pressures. This inner strength comes when a heart has been spiritually renewed. Knowing our identity and embracing how much God loves us allow our hearts to become vessels for this divine flow.

- *Genuine beauty is more valuable than superficial beauty.*
- *It takes a unique and rare quality to nurture inner beauty.*
- *This amazing strength comes when the heart is spiritually renewed.*

Like physical exercise, the greatest benefits of beauty starts within. This genuine quality involves our personality, thoughts, attitude, motives, actions, and the words we speak. Our inner self should be transformed daily to reflect God's characteristics in our lives—His love, joy, peace, hope, strength, patience, gentleness, goodness, and kindness. The quiet force of inner beauty is so powerful. God's Spirit transforms our lives to change from the inside out. It positively influences our outside world to make a difference in the lives of others.

- *Outer beauty fades in time; genuine beauty enhances in time.*
- *The quiet force of inner beauty transforms our lives.*
- *The quite force of inner beauty positively influence our outside world.*

A "quiet" and "gentle" spirit is not characterized by a mild or quiet personality or disposition. There is a significant difference. The attitude of the *inner self* determines the true state of a person's heart. A quiet spirit possesses the excellent and unselfish qualities that include caring about what matters most to God. People matter most to God. Therefore a quiet and gentle spirit reflects a kind, loving, sincere, and caring heart.

- *The attitude of the inner spirit reflects the true state of a person's heart.*
- *A quiet spirit reflects a kind, loving, sincere and loving heart.*

The priceless quality of real beauty cannot be obtained from the best workout regimen, a diet plan, plastic surgeries, or wearing the best hairstyle, make-up, designer clothes or jewelry. It reflects a sincere nature that comes from God alone. This inner quality is not popularly sought after in our culture. Therefore, it takes great conviction, faith and courage to stand for real beauty.

- *Real beauty cannot be obtained from the best workout, diet plan, clothes or jewelry.*
- *It takes great conviction, faith, and courage to stand for real beauty.*

Society tends to naturally work from the outside inward. But people can easily change their outer appearance while still struggling with inner turmoil. True intents and motives can be camouflaged for a period of time by appearance, words, and actions. But absolutely nothing is ever hidden from God at any time. He sees all things and knows all things. And the incorruptible attribute of genuine beauty is precious in *His* sight.

God is no respecter of persons. He created all women to manifest this beautiful quality within. He never intended for women to struggle with the insecurities that separate, divide and destroy relationships and prevent others from occurring. The petty rivalries, envy, gossiping, jealousy, backbiting and criticizing were never part of His original design. This historical trauma has passed down to generations. But it is time to break the hate. Today we are free to embrace the beauty in each other differences and be all that God created us to be.

The Bible is clear that we were fearfully and wonderfully made by God. Therefore, the variety of complexions, hair types, eye colors, body shapes and sizes express the beauty in God's creativity. If we change our view and see our creation as a wonderful masterpiece of His love; we would embrace our differences. To the contrary, societal influences tell us what we should look like, dress like and be like. Therefore, many people are discouraged when they do not measure up to these images. Women should pursue genuine beauty, not so much to have the perfect body, clothes, or appearance. Our countenance should shine bright to reflect our confidence and hope in our beautiful and amazing Creator.

- *Women should shine bright to reflect our hope in our beautiful Creator.*

A woman exercising real beauty to fulfill a divine purpose
I cannot discuss real beauty without sharing one of my favorite biblical stories. It eloquently illustrates a woman who exercised real beauty to fulfill her God-given purpose. I encourage you to read the entire story of Esther for yourself when you get a chance. Like Joseph's story, we learn many life lessons and how to overcome the games that haters play. What I find most interesting about this story is that the name "G-o-d" is unseen in this book of the Bible. But the life-changing, enemy-crushing hand of God is ever present. As a person's fingerprints confirm his or her identity, as you read this story, you know that God's mighty hand was at work. There is no other way this story could have taken place without His presence, power and favor.

Esther is an unknown orphan girl who God transforms into a woman of greatness. God takes an ordinary Jewish girl and prepares her to be a queen. A "hater" of the Jewish people, deceived the king and concocted a plan to annihilate Esther's people. But Esther's beautiful qualities within would gain her favor with the king to save an entire nation of people.

As events unfold, it is evident that God had a wonderful plan from the beginning of Esther's life. Esther's story gives us hope. There are times in our lives when it seems like God is not present or He doesn't see what we are going through. But this story is an excellent example of how He is always present. When we least expect it, He is working behind the scenes. As you see the circumstances surrounding this story, it is obvious that none of the events took place by chance. Each event was essential for God's greater plan for Esther's purpose.

Esther was given physical beauty for a reason. Like gifts and talents, physical beauty can be used to take others where God wants to use them. We see this in Esther's case. When it was time for the king to search for a new queen, physical beauty got Esther into the palace. But once she arrived, there were hundreds of beautiful women. All of the beautiful women of the land were gathered and taken to the palace. Physical beauty got the women in the competition, but it would take much more to be chosen as a queen.

When the women arrived at the palace, they didn't immediately go before the king. They had an extensive preparation process. For an entire year they were prepared with expensive cosmetics and treatments to beautify women and enhance their natural beauty. They were pampered and soaked in perform oils. Their diet was essential for good health and beauty. So they ate special foods to nourish the body and beautify the skin, nails and hair.

Learning palace etiquette was part of the preparation process. The women were instructed how to conduct themselves in the presence of the king. They would learn how to rise in the presence of the king, when to bow and when to approach the king. They learned when to speak and when to remain silent. Then their old clothes were removed, thrown away and most likely burned. The woman who would be chosen as queen would wear royal robes to signify her rich inheritance of the throne. They endured extensive training for their appearance, speech, elegance and countenance to signify royalty.

As women of God, He wants to remove issues in our hearts that prevent us from embracing His best for our lives. In the midst of a culture obsessed with outer appearance, God wants to set us apart for Himself. And with His help we can overcome society's pressures. This is the case in Esther's story. She faced daily competition, female rivalry, and distention among hundreds of beautiful women. Yet, she did not succumb to her daily environment. She rose above it. The best looking women and the most intense competition did not define her beauty. She had more than a pretty face and an attractive body. She set the standard for real beauty. But it would be wrapped in a royal package.

God wants to prepare all of His women as precious treasures. Like Esther, we should stand in a class all by ourselves. Without a word, our countenance and character should signify high standards. And we should know that our real worth and value cannot be found on the outside. We don't have to compete with other women or tear down their physical attributes. Even when it happens to us, we *can* rise above it.

Esther found favor with everyone who came in her presence. And she stood in a class all by herself. During her preparation, seven choice maidservants were provided from the king's palace. These women served in the king's palace and Esther and these ladies were moved to the best place in the house. Not only that, they knew palace etiquette. Therefore, they could coach Esther as she prepared to go before the king. And the stakes were very high.

After each woman's year of preparation, she would spend a night with the king. In the morning, instead of returning to the first house with women who were being prepared, she would go to the second house for women. If rejected, she would live a secluded and boring life. She could not return to her family or have a husband or family of her own. She would become a concubine. Concubines were set aside for sexual gratification. There were many concubines, but there could only be one queen.

When it was Esther's time to go before the king, she did not bring items to impress the king like the other women. They brought whatever they desired to enhance their physical beauty. Esther did not focus on all of the superficial things that the other women thought would gain the title. She took the advice of the person the king assigned to prepare the women. Today, God's Word and precious Spirit teach us how to be godly women. They reveal how to present ourselves as women of royalty and divine design.

The other women relied on their natural beauty, superficial clothing and ornaments and possibly their sexual appeal. But Esther had the wisdom to know a king would want much more than that for a lifetime commitment of mutual love and respect. Not only was her physical image considered, her whole being was critical to fulfill this great role and responsibility.

Esther would one day face the most difficult decision in her life. She would be placed in a position to put her life on the line for her people. Therefore, God was preparing her to be a woman of great faith. She would one day willingly put her desires to the side to look out for the best interest of others. Her humility, wisdom and great faith would allow her to make decisions that would affect lives of a nation. As women, each of us has a nation. There is a group of people who need to hear your story. There is a group of people who need to know how God has kept you and has brought you out. Your disappointments, hurt and pain are not in vain. God is preparing you to be a blessing to many others.

When the king encountered Esther, her physical beauty caught his attention. But her inner qualities captivated his heart. He was so delighted and pleased, that he loved her more than any of the women. Esther's countenance, character, wisdom, and humility gained the respect of the king. She had more than a beautiful image. Her genuine heart made the difference and a crown was placed on her head. The crown signified her position of royalty and honor.

This woman of integrity and elegance refused to be a concubine. A concubine tries to gain a king's attention by accentuating her physical attributes and focusing on superficial beauty to appeal to his sexual desire. A queen captures his heart and gain his love by her priceless qualities within. A concubine lives in the second house and shares space with other women as second class citizens. A queen lives in the best place and is surrounded by favor to meet all of her needs. A concubine spends the rest of her life waiting and wondering if she will ever be called again or by name. The queen is a woman of great respect and dignity and her name is known throughout the land.

Esther was different than all of the other women. And she stood out from the crowd. The king realized her price was far above rubies and he wanted to share all that he had with his godly bride. The king was so excited about finding his new queen. He planned a great celebration in her honor and the feast was named after Esther. He went as far to declare a holiday and gave gifts to all of the people in the land.

Esther did not begin her walk as a queen. But she was born to be a queen. She would become the most influential woman in the kingdom. Who would have imagined that an orphan girl, an exile from a foreign land whose people were despised and sought to be killed, would become the queen of a great nation? Esther's story clearly shows that how we are born, does not dictate who we will become. Like Esther, we don't start out as queens. But God sets us aside for Himself. Then with His guidance, we go through a preparation process. His Spirit transforms our lives from the inside out.

We change in every area of our lives to walk in divine royalty, to be used in ways we never imagined.

God set Esther on the throne and put her in position for His people. As a virtuous woman of God she possessed the unselfish qualities of deeply caring for the best interest of others. And at God's appointed time, this passionate, beautiful, bold woman of faith saved an entire nation of people from being unjustly slaughtered. Their hater deceived the king and plotted to kill Esther's people. But God intervened and the hater's plan backfired. Those who attempted to destroy her people were defeated at the end.

As we see in this story, gifts can take people to high places. But gifts don't make you popular with God. Hundreds of beautiful women made it to the palace. But Esther's godly character made her a queen. Her sincere heart for others brought her great success. It is the same today. People naturally look at the outside appearance, but God looks at the heart. Esther exercised real beauty. Her inner qualities shined so bright, that people of the heathen nation recognized the rare quality that comes from God alone.

Esther was an orphan girl who knew the pain of feeling abandoned and alone. And she knew from first-hand experience the pain of being hated because of cultural differences. But she exercised real beauty and looked out for the best interest of others. Are you willing to get over you, so God can use you? God allows us to go through the hater games to help others overcome. God wants to raise a high standard of women who will rise about the hate.

Are you ready to exercise real beauty? Are you ready to provoke women everywhere to exercise this magnificent quality within? This divine glow allows a little bit of heaven to shine on earth. And when real beauty radiates from the inside out, others will recognize God's amazing goodness in your life. It's your time to shine. Proverbs 31:30 says, *"Charm is deceitful and beauty is passing, but a woman who fears the Lord, she shall be praised."*

Step #5 Activity
Answer the following questions:

1. How would you describe outer beauty?

2. How would you define real beauty?

3. Name three things you like about your physical appearance.

4. Name two things you would change about your appearance.

5. How do you think the changes will make you feel? Why?

6. What life lessons can we learn from Esther's story?

7. Describe your real beauty within.

8. How would you describe a concubine in today's times?

9. What are characteristics of a godly bride?

10. How can you become a woman of divine royalty?

STEP 6

AIM TO
EAT RIGHT

Today, experts agree that the definition of health includes a person's total well-being—spiritually, physically, psychologically, socially and mentally. It includes one's emotional state and being free from anxiety, stress and depression, or overcoming these obstacles through healthy lifestyle practices. Good health includes minimizing the risk of illnesses and diseases to live a better quality of life.

Like an athlete trains to win, overcoming the hater games requires taking care of our health. The healthier we are, the better we can focus on our goals, overcome life challenges and fulfill our purpose to the best of our ability. A healthy person is able to carry out their daily activities with ease. Healthy people have a more positive outlook on life and have ample energy to enjoy the most important things in life. Total health includes all aspects of a person's life.

Of course our spiritual well-being is more important. It affects us now and in the life to come. But no matter how spiritual we are, neglect of the body leads to premature physical deterioration and health consequences. 3 John 2 says, *"Beloved, I pray that you may prosper in all things and be in health, just as your soul prospers."* God cares about our total health. Therefore, we need to properly care for the physical and emotional needs of the body. The body, spirit and soul are connected. They are intertwined and they work hand-in-hand. If one is out of balance, it affects the whole person. Plus there is only one you. And God gave you one body to live out this one life. When we take care of our body, we are able to express our lives with the vitality that brings honor to God. Some situations are beyond our control. For instance, some people have medical conditions or take medication that affect their ability to exercise or contribute to weight gain. But we can do our best where we are and with the resources we have available. Then trust God with the rest.

Healthy living is not a size issue. It is a health issue. Your body size or weight is a problem when it increases your risk for illnesses and diseases, drains your energy, and inhibits your ability to perform your daily activities. Let me make this clear: **God loves you regardless of your body size.** You were fearfully and wonderfully made in His eyes. In His divine creativity, He did not create us to have the same body shape, size or frame. Everyone was not created to be a size 2, 4, 6 or 8.

If God created you to be a size 10, 12, 14, or higher, have confidence in the beautiful masterpiece He created you to be. What's important is to strive for good health. Contrary to what many people believe, a person who is small in size is not necessarily fit and healthy. Obesity is only one risk factor that contributes to diseases. People who are naturally thin or small still need exercise for a healthy heart and proper nutrition for optimum health and disease protection.

Year after year, many people strive to lose weight. But the focus should be good health. Losing weight is not a problem for many people. We can lose weight on almost any diet. The real problem is losing weight the healthy way and keeping it off by maintaining a healthy lifestyle. Fad diets promise quick weight loss, but they affect you in different ways. Eliminating certain foods from your diet can decrease your energy level. Plus depriving yourself of your favorite foods can make you cranky and intensify cravings. Many people who restrict their diets find themselves binging later. Plus losing weight too quickly results in losing water and lean muscle tissue, which causes fatigue and an unhealthy appearance. Another problem is that many dieters gain back more weight than they actually lost.

When our cars or appliances break down, we go to the manufacturer or the person qualified to repair these items. For proper functioning of the body, we should consider the One who created our bodies. Many of the problems associated with obesity and diseases could be prevented or the risk greatly decreased by understanding God's original plan. He created the human body to require ingredients from natural foods to function properly and for optimum health. The vegetation on the earth was created to sustain our lives. Therefore, all of the food we eat comes from plants. Bread and pasta are made from kernels of wheat. They start out as green grass that dries out in the sun and change color to a golden brown. The grains we eat all come from the seeds of grasses. So whenever you eat a slice of bread, a bowl of spaghetti, or a sandwich, just remember that grass from the earth made it possible.

However, today, we don't have to wonder why the acronym for the "standard American diet" is "sad". More than ever, people eat more refined, calorie-rich foods that have been stripped of their nutrients and fiber. These foods have replaced natural foods such as whole-grain breads, pasta, and rice, and beans. Many people consume a good deal of calories through highly processed, convenient foods loaded with fats and sugars. There is some truth to "You are what you eat." Too much of the wrong foods and not enough good choices lead to poor health. Nutrition is critical for your body to fight illnesses and diseases and to naturally heal and repair itself. In addition, certain food choices contribute to bodily aches and pains and joint inflammation. Food also affects people suffering with certain mood disorders, depression, and PMS. Their daily diet can minimize or exacerbate the symptoms.

Plus the food we eat affects our overall mood and attitude. Have you eaten a heavy meal and felt tired and sluggish and ready to take a nap? Or you feel this way after eating high-fat foods. Unhealthy choices are more taxing on the digestive system, making it work harder. The result is feeling sluggish. Eating heavy foods late at night makes you wake up feeling hung over.. Or when you eat a sugary snack you immediately feel full of energy and then crash and feel the blues later. Some people feel this way after they eat chocolate or drink a caffeinated beverage such as soda or coffee. They initially feel charged and then become irritable or energy-depleted later. These examples show some of the ways why the food we consume is critical for our day-to-day functioning.

Times have truly changed. A major problem is many of the foods we eat today are not what God originally created for optimum health. Our bodies were not created to process all of the extra calories, fat, sodium, sugar, and artificial and synthetic ingredients that are put into foods. They are wearing down the body's ability to metabolize or break down all of the extra sugars and calories. In turn, they contribute to the high rate of heart disease, obesity, diabetes, high cholesterol, high blood pressure, certain cancers and other illnesses. If you already have heart disease, diabetes, or another medical condition, it is more critical to eat a healthier diet. It's not too late to start.

We live in a fast-paced society in which unhealthy food is everywhere. We cannot escape the temptation. When you turn on the television late at night you see it. The temptation leads you to search for an evening snack that is either sweet or crunchy. When you open magazines you see advertisements of poor choices. When you drive down the road, fast food signs are everywhere. When you walk in the mall, the smell of pastries calls your name. So it is so easy to make unhealthy choices.

In addition, we work longer hours or have other commitments. We feel as though we have too much to do and too little time to do it. Time constraints affect our ability to make good food choices. In the hustle and bustle of our everyday lives it is challenging to focus on healthy meal preparation for the family. Quick-fix meals are more appealing, as they fit into a busy schedule. Microwavable meals and high-salt, high-fat meals are available in a can, box or bag. We order in and out. Fast food restaurants offer two for the price of one special, supersize meals and the dollar menu. Everything is oversized and "all you can eat" specials at restaurants advertise more for less. These deals make it so tempting to settle for unhealthy choices.

Then we all can agree that food is very important during social events. Nothing is wrong with getting together and eating. But it is the types of foods that are prepared. It is normal to see a church spread that includes high fat foods such as fried chicken and foods loaded with fat, butter and sauces. There are deserts such as cakes, pastries, pies, soda and other sugary drinks. When you see a vegetable, it is often loaded with a high fat meat to add flavor. Bake sales and fundraisers display high-fat foods and high sugary snacks.

On the job it is not unusual for managers to bring donuts and pastries for breakfast for their employees; where bagels, fruit or yogurt would be a better choice. Or they may treat employees with a pizza party instead of turkey wraps or a healthier alternative. To drink, they have several liters of soda on hand. On top of this, many manufacturers place profit over people. They load the grocery store shelves with so many unhealthy choices. Many of these foods and fast foods have been processed and stripped of all of the good stuff such as vitamins, minerals and fiber that promote good health. They are loaded with bad stuff. All of these options result in eating too many foods loaded with calories, fat, sodium, and sugar. Eating these unhealthy choices regularly are a big part of the problem. Research indicates there is a direct relationship between diet and disease.

We cannot blame our busy schedules, the manufacturers or our environments for poor choices. We have the responsibility to be good stewards of our bodies and the precious gift of life God has given us. We have to take charge of our health. Getting the knowledge will help you make better choices. And yes, it seems difficult because of our schedules, the convenience of unhealthy foods and the stores are loaded with them. The truth is healthier choices can take a little longer to prepare. But in the long-run the time is worth the sacrifice. Healthier foods provide nutrients for good health and give you more energy to perform better at home, work, church, recreation and wherever you go. Good nutrition helps you feel better, look better and improve your energy level. If we really want to win at life, we have to aim to eat right.

The body needs a variety of foods from all five food groups to ensure proper nutrition for our total well-being. Eating foods rich in nutrients and fiber satisfies the body; unlike nutrient-poor foods that cause you to overeat. These unhealthy choices are depleted of the nutrients and fiber that feed the body and satisfy our hunger. Getting sufficient vitamins and minerals is important for proper functioning and healing of the body. Food was meant to be enjoyed and to nourish the body to function at its best.

We have to make a deliberate effort and plan to eat healthier to reach our goals. This includes making better food selections in the grocery store, in restaurants, at fast food locations and during meal preparations at home. Healthy eating does not mean to exclude all of your favorite foods. Most foods can fit into a healthy diet when eaten in moderation. The problem is people often over eat the unhealthy choices. Therefore we have to make an effort to aim for our target daily.

Most of our daily caloric intake should come from whole grains, fruits, vegetables, beans, nuts and seeds. Not all of the substances in food have been discovered yet. So when you eat the natural foods from the earth, you're getting the good stuff we know about and the good stuff that we don't know about yet. People tend to focus on the outside of the body, but God created the body by divine design. The body was created to naturally heal itself, protect itself, to fight against diseases and toxins, to preserve life, and to naturally clean and detoxify itself. Your immune system is constantly working to fight against potential threats of illnesses and diseases. As soon as you start to get sick, an entire rescue squad of white blood cells attack the foreign matter. All day long your body is getting rid of waste to prevent it from accumulating and poisoning your body. The nutrients in food makes it all happen.

When you go on a fad diet and limit certain foods, you are depriving your body of all the good stuff it needs for optimum health and performance. Therefore, fad dieting is not the answer. The answer is to take charge of our health. We can be our own health advocate and get the right information to eat better. With so many choices in grocery stores and with so many foods that have been manipulated by manufacturers, how do you know what you are getting? We have to learn more about the food we eat. We cannot remain ignorant of something so intimate as the Word of God to strengthen our spiritual health. In the same manner, we cannot remain ignorant of something so critical as the food we eat which affects our physical well-being.

Food does for the body, what the Word of God does for the soul. Natural foods and drinking plenty of water naturally detoxify the body as God's Word and Holy Spirit detoxify the soul. The Word of God strengthens our inner beings and prevents spiritual blockages of the heart. Nutritious foods strengthen the body and reduce the risk of illnesses, including the number-one killer, heart disease. The Word of God sustains our spirit and helps us grow. Nutritious foods nourish the body to improve our overall physical well-being. The uncompromising Word of God heals us and protects us from destructions in this life. Substances such as vitamins and minerals in natural foods protect the body and help it naturally heal. We need the entire message in the Word of God in its proper context for optimum spiritual health and growth. For optimum health and disease prevention the body needs foods from all five food groups (grains, vegetables, fruits, milk, meat, and beans) to feel satisfied and to function at its' best.

Have you ever wondered why it is so easy to overeat junk food? Or have you ever thought about why you cannot get satisfied when you eat unhealthier choices? It is so easy to overeat processed foods and junk foods because the body is still hungry. Fiber and vital nutrients have been stripped which are necessary for the body to be nutritiously fed and to feel satisfied. As the whole message in God's Word builds a strong inner life and satisfies the soul, there are six basic nutrients that are needed to maintain satiety, proper healing and functioning of the body. Fiber is not really a nutrient.

It is included in this list because it serves a very important role in the diet. This basic nutrition information will help you understand why the food we eat is so important. The following list contains the essential building materials for a healthy temple:

1. **Water**: Water is the most abundant and most important resource on the earth. It is the most basic nutrient needed by the body and has many functions. Many natural foods such as fruits and vegetables contain plenty of water. Some vegetables and fruits can have up to 95% water. Even dry foods contain some water. However, drinking plain water is your best source. Unless you have a dry throat or sweat running down your brow, you probably take it for granted. The recommendation is at least eight, 8-ounce glasses per day. One of the most important things you can do for your body is to drink plenty of water. And water does a lot more than satisfy your thirst.

Without water there will be no life on earth. The human body can survive weeks without food, but only days without water. God created man from the dust of the earth, but He created the human body with over half of its body weight from water. The body does not have a water cycle like the earth. We have to constantly replenish the body's water supply throughout the day to keep the body functioning properly and to meet the body's needs. The lack of water can have a serious impact on our health. Failure to replenish the body with sufficient water can result in dehydration, fatigue, heat exhaustion, muscle cramps, and poor performance.

A major problem with quick-fix diet plans is losing water, which can lead to dehydration. The weight loss is only temporary and the body will fight to try to get it back quickly. Exercising in a rubber suit or a sauna to lose weight is not an effective weight loss method either. Sweat is critical for regulating the body's temperature and cooling off the body. The sweat must be able to evaporate from the skin to avoid heat stress disorders. If for some reason you lose weight from sweating, you need to replace the water loss as soon as possible. Dehydration can lead to serious fluid loss, which could be fatal if not treated immediately. Symptoms include fatigue, dizziness, headaches, extreme thirst, increased body temperature, nausea and confusion.

Drinking plenty of water helps with weight loss. Drinking water between meals and during meals can also help you eat less. When you are hungry it can take up to 15 to 20 minutes for the body to realize that you have eaten. Many people tend to overeat because they eat too fast. By the time the body realizes they have eaten, they have *over*eaten and feel stuffed. Drinking water during a meal helps slow you down so that the body can realize it has eaten to avoid overeating.

In some instances, when you have eaten and you still feel hungry, you could actually be thirsty. Many people mix these two signals. If you drink a glass of water the feeling of hunger may subside. Before I developed the habit of drinking water, I drank high-calorie beverages if I was thirsty. Usually it was a sugary juice drink, whole milk, or a soda. Today I know not to reach for drinks like soda, fruit cocktails, Kool-Aid, and coffee to quench my thirst. Unfortunately many people fail to drink enough fluid and when they do it's often the wrong type of fluid. Although these beverages contain water, none of them are as good as the real thing. When you drink plain old water, your body doesn't have to process the sugars, artificial sweeteners, or chemicals found in other drinks. Your body gets all of the wonderful benefits without all of the extra work. Water is also low in sodium, has no caffeine, has no calories, and acts as a natural laxative.

A good way to tell if you are getting sufficient water is by the color of your urine. Clear or pale yellow urine indicates a sufficient water intake. Dark yellow or orangey urine definitely indicates you are not drinking enough water unless you are taking vitamins or medications that affect the color. As you begin to drink more water you may notice a very natural response: You will get the urge to urinate more frequently. However, the frequency will subside as your body adapts to the additional fluids.

Understanding calories the way I do today, I understand why I gained so much weight in the past. One cup of whole milk has 150 calories and some of the sugary drinks and juices have about 120 calories per cup or more. Although 100% juice is fine, you still have to be careful of not drinking too many cups of juice. Some contain artificial ingredients and sugars and the calories per cup can add up. Extra calories in the body are stored as extra fat on the body. Eating the fruit is a much better choice. Drinking more water can also help you cut back on sodas and other high-calorie drinks.

There are many people who drink sodas throughout the day. One description of soda is "liquid candy." Soda provides absolutely no nutrients for the body. It provides extra calories and often contains caffeine. Caffeinated beverages are not a good source for fluid because caffeine has a diuretic effect, which actually increases water loss. Drinks containing alcohol can also contribute to dehydration. Studies have shown that sodas and sugary drinks play a large role in obesity among adults and children because of all of the extra calories. Sugary drinks and colas also contribute to cavities in children because they are loaded with sugars and sweeteners. Diet colas are low in calories, but contain artificial ingredients that are not good for the body. The bottom line is water is the best drink. Water is so important for our existence and health that

Jesus Christ refers to Himself as "living water" in the Bible. Have you had your "glory" today?

2. **Carbohydrates**: Carbohydrates supply the fuel or energy to move, think, and operate effectively and efficiently. Did you ever go a period of time without eating and felt light-headed, dizzy, irritated or got a head ache? This may have occurred because your body ran out of fuel. Foods such as grains, cereals, nuts, vegetables, fruits and legumes are all part of plants and supply the body with energy. The complex carbohydrates from whole-grains (such as bread, pasta), corn, rice, beans, and potatoes provide the body with important nutrients and fiber. Fruit, a simple sugar, also supplies the body with important nutrients. Both sugars and starches supply the body with four calories per gram of carbohydrate.

Unfortunately, the starches—such as bread, pasta and rice have been falsely labeled as the dieter's nightmare. Some vegetables like the baked potato or sweet potato contain a high percentage of carbohydrates and have also been mislabeled. Many people try to avoid these carbohydrate-rich foods when they want to lose weight. Contrary to what many people believe, these foods are loaded with the necessary vitamins, minerals and fiber to keep the body functioning properly and minimizing the risk for disease and illness. You should limit your intake of sugar in your diet, but complex carbohydrates such as wholegrain products, rice and beans provide the body with energy and they are excellent sources of vitamins, minerals and fiber for good health.

If we are honest with ourselves, the real problem is not the food. Many people eat too many carbohydrates, eat large serving sizes and smother the food with all of the butter, sour cream, gravies, and sauces that add on the extra calories. Countries where complex carbohydrates are the primary source of food do not suffer with the epidemic of obesity and heart disease like we see in this country. Clearly, eating carbohydrates is not the cause of obesity and should not be excluded from the diet.

3. **Protein**: Protein makes up every living cell in the body. Therefore, protein is known as the building material of the body. Protein repairs body cells as they are damaged or wear out and builds and repairs muscle tissue. Protein helps regulate body processes and acts as antibodies to protect you from bacteria and viruses that cause illness and disease. Protein supplies you with energy if you don't consume enough carbohydrates. However, eating adequate carbohydrates saves the protein so it can perform its important function to repair and build body tissue. Protein is very important for health and weight management, as are all nutrients. Since protein is responsible for building muscle tissue, it helps you have a strong, firm, healthy body.

Animal proteins have been labeled as the best source of protein. They contain all of the essential amino acids which are the building blocks for proteins. However, the concern with eating too many animal foods is fat. Meat has a higher fat and cholesterol content than foods of plant origin. Good protein sources include lean meats, poultry, fish, and eggs. Animal proteins are not the only source of protein.

Vegetarians get sufficient protein by eating a variety of vegetables, grains, legumes, nuts, seeds and fruit. The body needs the combination of amino acids in these foods for a complete protein. If an amino acid is lacking in one food you can get it from another. Eating a variety of foods is the key. Good plant sources of protein include nuts, peanut butter, tofu, hummus and beans. In addition to eating a variety of foods, you can combine foods to create a complete protein: a peanut butter sandwich, pasta and cheese, beans and rice, milk and cereal, a cheese sandwich, and a tortilla and beans are good combinations. Like carbohydrates, protein also contains four calories per gram.

4. **Fat:** "Fat" is not a bad word. Fat has a bad connotation because of our concern with being overweight. But fat is an essential nutrient. You cannot live without. Fat has many important roles in the body. It carries the fat-soluble vitamins, A, D, E and K through the bloodstream to nourish the body. Fat combines with other nutrients to form important compounds in the body. It is an essential component of the body's cell walls.

Certain fatty acids help children grow properly and are needed for adults to have healthy skin. It provides insulation for the body and helps protect and cushion our internal organs from injuries and strengthen our joints. It aids in hormone production and helps absorption of the fat soluble vitamins. It also enhances the taste of food by adding a good flavor and texture, and fat helps us feel full. Fat also supplies the body with energy during physical activity.

Fat itself is not a problem when it comes to being overweight. The problems is consuming too many high-fat or high-calorie foods. If you do not burn off the extra energy through physical activity it will be stored on the body as extra fat. A major benefit of eating a diet rich in fruits, vegetables, and whole grains is that these foods are naturally low in fat. Animal fats are generally high in saturated fat which can contribute to heart disease. Meat products can also be high in cholesterol, which in excess can contribute to illness. Saturated fats are also found in dairy products.

Excessive fat in the diet is a major cause of obesity and can contribute to heart disease, certain cancers, diabetes, hypertension and other illnesses. One gram of fat has more than twice the calories of a gram of carbohydrate or protein. Fat has nine calories per gram compared to the four calories of carbohydrates and protein. It is important to read food labels to avoid foods high in fats and foods made with hydrogenated fats. "Hydrogenation" is a process where otherwise healthy fat has been made unhealthy to promote the shelf life of certain processed or prepared foods such as snack crackers.

5. **Vitamins**: Vitamins are critical for life, as the root word "vita" indicates and they are naturally found in non-processed foods. Vitamins do not provide the body with any energy, but they are essential for good health and disease prevention. Vitamins are readily available in the foods we eat and are only needed in minute quantities. The 13 Vitamins are divided into two main groups: fat soluble—vitamins A, D, E and K and water soluble—vitamins C and B complex.

Vitamins have many functions in the body. They regulate the chemical processes within the body and without them the body will not function properly. For instance, Vitamin A is vital for healthy skin, bones, teeth and vision. It is found in leafy green vegetables, orange fruits and vegetables, eggs, liver, and cream or butter. Vitamin D is necessary for healthy bone and for the retention of calcium. It is found in fish oil, liver and eggs and is made through the body's exposure to sunlight. Vitamin E is an antioxidant that can protect the body from disease. It is found in wheat germ, green leafy vegetables, and vegetable oils. It is mainly stored in body fat. Vitamin K is mainly for blood coagulation and is found in green leafy vegetables, eggs, soybean oil, alfalfa and liver.

Vitamin C enhances the immune system and protects you from diseases and illnesses. Many fruits such as oranges, grapefruits, strawberries, tangerines, kiwi, and cantaloupe are good sources of the antioxidant vitamin C. Vegetables are excellent sources of vitamin C and beta-carotene in addition to many other nutrients. The B vitamins are known as the B complex and include: thiamin (B1), riboflavin (B2), niacin (B3), pyridoxine (B6), cyanocobalamin (B12), folic acid, pantothenic acid and biotin. The B complex vitamins are essential for metabolic reactions within the body, help with metabolism of food and allow other vital reactions to take place within the body. These vitamins also serve as antioxidants which help prevent diseases.

Vitamins perform a broad range of functions in the body. They ensure that our immune system functions at its best to protect us from illnesses and diseases and help the body's overall performance. The body does not manufacture most vitamins. It is important to get vitamins from eating a variety of natural foods. Vitamins are best when absorbed from natural foods that are eaten rather than from supplements. Vitamin supplements should not be a substitute for eating a healthy diet. Many nutritionists believe that the naturally occurring micronutrients in food are important to ensure we get everything the body needs for good health. Fruits, vegetables and whole grains are loaded with vitamins.

Vegetables generally have a higher nutritional content than fruits and also contain phytochemicals and other substances found in plants that protect us from disease. Cruciferous vegetables or those in the cabbage family, such as cabbage, cauliflower, kale, broccoli, collards, and others are believed to protect from cancer. The deep green and yellow vegetables such as broccoli, spinach, carrots and sweet potatoes, have more beta-carotene. Whole grains such as whole wheat bread and brown rice and other whole grain products such as wheat germ and cereals are excellent sources of the B vitamins. Whole grains, as well as nuts—another plant food—also contain the antioxidant vitamin E that protects the body from disease. That's why it's important to make sure you eat a variety of foods to get an adequate supply of all of the necessary vitamins for good health.

6. **Minerals**: When you hear the word "mineral" you may think about rocks in the earth. But minerals are also essential for life and good health. Like vitamins, minerals help regulate many bodily functions. They are responsible for a number of biological reactions in the body such as the assimilation of nutrients, fluid balance, muscle contraction, nerve impulses, hormone production, and digestion. They also contribute to body structure. There are two classifications of minerals: major minerals or "macrominerals," and trace minerals.

The major minerals are not more important than the trace minerals. They are just needed in greater amounts in the body. Major minerals include calcium, magnesium, phosphorous, and potassium. Trace minerals include chromium, copper, iodine, iron, and manganese. Looking at minerals we can clearly see God's wisdom in planning. Not only do minerals help regulate bodily processes, but they also help form structures in the body.

In Genesis, Chapter 1, God created man from the earth. God also brought forth plants from the earth. Minerals are inorganic. They are not made through living organisms and they originate from the earth. Plants use minerals from the soil to help them create the food they need to grow. In turn we eat the plant foods that contain minerals in order for our bodies to grow and function properly. Or we eat the animals that eat the plants that obtained their minerals from the soil. An example of this is the calcium that forms bone and teeth.

Calcium is also involved in muscle contractions, blood clotting, enzyme activity and nerve transmission in the body. Although dairy products such as milk, cheese and yogurt are rich sources of calcium, calcium is also found in green vegetables such as broccoli, bok choy, and kale. Many juices such as orange juice are now fortified with calcium. Osteoporosis, a disease that causes weakness of the bone, making bones more susceptible to fractures, is caused by a deficiency of calcium.

Iron, another important mineral, is an essential part of hemoglobin that carries oxygen-rich blood to every cell in your body. You may have heard of anemia or iron deficiency, especially in women. Iron is found in foods of animal origin and plant origin. Some good plant sources of iron are soybeans, peas, whole grain breads and cereals, leafy green vegetables, such as spinach, red kidney beans, lima beans and prune juice. Refined foods contain hardly any minerals. Eating a well-balanced diet with a variety of foods can help you get the minerals the body needs to function properly.

7. **Fiber:** Whole grains, fruits and vegetables are easily digested, pass through the body quickly and are rich in fiber which aids in elimination and natural detoxification. Processed foods and refined products stays in the body longer and can contribute to constipation. Although fiber is necessary for good health, it is not a nutrient like carbohydrate, protein and fat. Fiber cannot be converted into energy, and it does not aid in the body processes like vitamins and minerals. Fiber helps reduce the risk of colon cancer and can lower blood cholesterol level. Fiber decreases constipation and increases regularity. It removes the stool and toxins from the body more quickly that can contribute to colon cancer.

Fiber is not digested by the body, but it is important for weight management and good health. Fiber also creates bulk, making you feel fuller, thereby eating less. Plenty of people eat too many processed foods. These foods have been stripped of the fiber that helps us to feel naturally satisfied after eating. We naturally over-eat unhealthy foods because they have been stripped of substances that feed the body. Plus studies have shown that people with a low-fiber diet have a higher risk for heart disease, certain cancers and other illnesses. Increasing your intake of fiber can decrease your risk of these illnesses.

Most Americans do not regularly consume enough fruits, vegetables or whole grains. How many servings of fruits, vegetables or whole grains have you had today? Yesterday? This week? It is not too late to add whole grain breads and cereals, fruits, vegetables, beans and bran cereals to your diet today. If fiber isn't part of your daily diet, you could be putting yourself at a greater risk for illnesses and increasing your risk for colon cancer. All that we do should bring honor to God, including the food and drinks we consume. We may not have control over everything, but we should thank God for our food and enjoy the wonderful variety He has provided. We can only do our best with the resources we have available and trust God to help us with the rest. Are you ready to use your resources to invest in your total health? Are you ready to make the change to reap the benefits of healthier eating?

Healthy eating tips to focus on your goals

If you are ready to make changes with you diet, make small gradual, realistic changes. Making too many changes at once will set you up for failure. Conquer one or two areas at a time then move on to another area in an order that is most comfortable for you. Do it with a goal in mind. And don't focus on the scale or become obsessed with your weight. That would be a huge distraction from staying focused on healthy lifestyle changes. I like to say, "When you strive to be fit, the look will be your tip".

The suggestions below are more than enough information for healthy eating. But remember, it took time to develop poor eating habits and it will take consistency and time to change them. You can set a goal of trying these tips in the order that they are presented or in another order that works best for you. According to psychologists, it takes at least twenty one days to create a habit. However long it takes you to make changes, be patient, determined and consistent. And if you feel as if you've messed up in a particular area, don't beat yourself up. This is a process. Don't get stuck in what you consider is a failure. A mistake is really an opportunity to learn and to grow. Just keep going. Don't stop. And you'll discover how eating healthier is important to help you win at life. The following tips will help you apply the knowledge in the previous list as you aim to eat right for a healthier life:

1. *Drink plenty of water.* Drink at least eight 8-ounce cups per day. As noted previously, water is the best thing going for your body. Limit your intake of sodas and caffeinated beverages which can cause you to lose more water and gain more weight. Other drinks contain some water, but there is nothing that can replace the real thing. When you drink water your body doesn't have to process all of the calories and artificial ingredients or sweeteners.

Tips for drinking more water

- *Start your day with a glass of water.* Just as you have a habit of brushing your teeth first thing in the morning, also start your day with a refreshing cup of water.
- *Drink water with meals and snacks.* Drinking water with meals and snacks and in between meals and snacks can help you eat less. It can also help ensure you're getting an adequate intake of water. Food should be supplemented with water to make sure the body maintains proper hydration. Your body uses its water to process food; therefore this water needs to be replaced.

- *Drink water when you normally would drink soda, coffee or caffeinated tea.* Caffeine has a diuretic effect, which actually causes the body to lose water through more frequent urination.
- *Take water breaks on your job.* We often get so busy on the job and don't take water breaks. This causes dehydration, which makes you feel fatigued and not function at your best.
- *Keep a bottle or cup of water at your desk to sip on.* This helps you avoid confusing the thirst signal with the hunger signal. If you don't drink enough water you could grab a snack thinking you're hungry when the body actually needs more fluids.
- *Treat yourself with flavored water.* This can be a better alternative for people making the switch from soft drinks. Add fruit slices like lemons, oranges or even lime in your water for a refreshing drink. Read the labels on flavored water because some of these waters contain a lot of sugar and artificial ingredients, which defeats the purpose of drinking pure water.
- *Travel with a bottle of water.* Traveling with water is a good way to prevent dehydration throughout the day and to ensure you're getting adequate water, especially during long periods in the car or when traveling by air.
- *Drink water before, during, and after exercise.* You need to drink at least four to six ounces of water every 15 to 20 minutes of exercising to prevent dehydration and muscle cramping.
- *Keep your body well hydrated in the summer.* Hot, humid weather causes your body to perspire more and therefore lose more water.
- *Keep your body well hydrated in the winter.* It's just as important to drink water during the winter as in the summer. During the winter we spend most of our time indoors where the heat evaporates the moisture in the skin.

   <u>*2. Eat plenty of fruits, vegetables and whole grains*</u>. These foods contain the many natural ingredients we know about and the ones we don't know about yet, for the body to be healthy and to function at its best. Variety is the key to ensure you're getting an adequate supply of all of the essential nutrients, including vitamins, minerals and fiber. Fruits and vegetables should be included in every meal and as snacks throughout the day. Eat a variety of fruits and vegetables, including more dark green leafy vegetables and add dry beans and peas to your diet. Choose whole grains--breads, crackers, pasta and rice--daily. Try snacking on healthy nut mixes, whole wheat pretzels or fruit instead of grabbing a bag of chips. Then when you fix a plate, fill half of it with fruits and vegetables.

   I believe God created fruit to satisfy man's sweet tooth. They naturally satisfy cravings to help us cut back on sugary snacks. Fruits are nature's fast foods. Keep fruit readily available to grab it as a snack or a quick pick-me-up. You can try it fresh, frozen, dried or canned (in its natural juice). You can also try real fruit smoothies as a healthier alternative to ice cream or shakes. However, go easy on fruit juices. The calories quickly add up (120 calories per 8-ounce cup) and some have artificial ingredients and sweeteners. The real fruit is a much better choice. Natural foods help you fill full or satisfied because they contain fiber. Selecting these more filling foods help you avoid over eating. Here are some ways to eat more fruits and vegetable:

- Top your cereal, yogurt or pancakes with fruit for breakfast.
- Drink a glass of orange juice with breakfast.
- Eat a medium size fruit such as an apple, pear, peach or banana for a snack.
- Snack on carrots or celery sticks during lunch.
- Snack on dried fruit instead of candy.

- Eat broccoli, spinach, or a salad with dinner.
- Create a fruit or vegetable salad or a combination as a snack or meal.
- Prepare a fruit smoothie as a snack or dessert.

3. *If God didn't make it, eat it sparingly.* A good rule of thumb is, if God created it and man manipulated it by stripping all of the good stuff and adding bad stuff, eat it sparingly. Or if God made it and man changed it, limit your intake. Many foods in the grocery store have been stripped of their natural fiber and nutrients through over processing. They have been changed by being loaded with fat, sugar, artificial ingredients and other chemicals that are not good for your health. Man took what God created for our good and manipulated it and changed it from its original state. Check the label to determine what's in it or what it is, in some instances.

Shopping on the outer aisles of grocery stores will help you make "real food" selections. When you eat a variety of real foods you don't have to worry about getting sufficient nutrients. Real foods include fruits, vegetables, meats, dairy, and whole grain breads. They are also good for weight management because they are naturally low in calories, fat, sodium, and sugars. Be aware: the inner aisles contain most of the unhealthier choices such as processed foods, high sodium foods, high-fat foods, and sugary snacks and drinks which are very tempting. You don't have to eliminate all of your favorites. They should be a small portion of your diet and eaten sparingly. And if you know you don't have control over a certain food, don't bring it home. Do the best you can with the resources and choices you have available. Budget your money, write a grocery list in advance and prioritize your spending. Do you best, trust God with the rest.

4. *Limit your intake of foods high in fat.* Watch your intake of high fat meats such as beef and pork. Try leaner portions of meat,

including chicken, turkey and fish. Be watchful of high fat dairy products, such as butter, cheese, whole milk and ice cream. Try the lighter versions or limit your intake. Limit frying foods, which adds significant fat and calories to foods. Try baking, grilling or roasting meats. Remember fat has more than twice the calories of carbohydrates and protein and can add on the extra pounds quickly.

Consuming too much fat and cholesterol contributes to coronary heart disease leading to heart attack or stroke. Studies have shown that the buildup of plaque in the arteries' walls begins as early as childhood. Therefore, this isn't just about you. Introduce your children to healthy eating too. The following lists can help you make better choices:

Making healthier meat selections

- Eat more lean poultry, turkey, and fish; and choose lean cuts of meat.
- Eat fish at least twice a week, but don't fry it.
- Trim all the visible fat from meats and remove the skin from poultry.
- Oven fry chicken and fish. Fried chicken is twice as fattening as baked.
- Bake, broil, roast, grill, oven-fry, stir-fry, sauté, or simmer meats.
- Limit your intake of processed meats; or try low-fat versions.
- Drain off the oil or fat from meat after cooking it.
- Instead of using pork to season foods, try smoked turkey pieces.
- Replace ground beef with ground turkey or mix turkey and lean beef.
- Select tuna packed in water instead of vegetable oil.
- Limit egg yolks to no more than three per week and use more egg whites.

Cutting fat and calories

- Whipped margarine or butter in tubs has less fat than the sticks.
- Go easy on the butter, sour cream and cream cheese, or use low-fat varieties.
- Top pancakes, waffles, or French toast with fruit or fruit spread instead of syrup.
- Limit salad dressing to 1 or 2 tablespoons, or use low-fat or fat-free versions.
- Limit intake of fried foods which can double calories.
- Limit intake of fast foods or select healthier options.
- At restaurants ask for salad dressing on the side to control the amount.
- God easy on gravies, sauces, and spreads.
- Try fruit spreads on toast or bread instead of butter or margarine.
- Try herbs, spices, and lemon to flavor meats instead of gravies, sauces, and fat drippings.
- Eat candy, pastries, cake, and other sweets in moderation.
- Limit intake of soft drinks and drink more water and 100% fruit juices.
- Replace sugary and fattening snacks and desserts with a variety of fresh fruit.
- Choose wholesome cereals that are low in sugar such at oatmeal or bran flakes.
- Eat a bagel for breakfast instead of donut or pastries.
- Go easy on adding extra sugar to foods. Try spices and fruit juices to add flavor.
- Try sherbet, frozen low-fat yogurt, ice milk, or frozen fruit bars instead of ice cream. However, watch out for low-fat claims which could be loaded with sugar.
- In recipes requiring milk, use skim or low-fat instead of whole milk.

- Try a frozen fruit smoothie instead of a milkshake, or create your own using fruit, juice or skim milk, and/or low-fat yogurt.

5. *Limit your intake of foods high in sugar.* Sugary snacks, sugary drinks, pastries, baked goods and candies contribute to the extra calories in the American diet that contributes to obesity and disease in adults, adolescents and children. All foods can be incorporated in a healthy diet plan and there are really no "bad" foods. The problem is we tend to overdo it and consume too much, too often. You don't have to exclude your favorite foods. These foods should be limited in your eating plan. You have to consider the health "cost" when you consume these foods. Most of them are "empty calorie" foods, which mean they provide the calories that add on the extra pounds while having little to no nutritional value for the health of your body. Consuming too many sugary snacks and drinks also contribute to cavities, tooth loss and even gum disease. According to studies, gum disease has been linked to heart disease.

6. *Limit your intake of foods high in sodium.* Sodium is important because it moves fluid in and out of the body's cells, it regulates blood pressure, transmits nerve impulses and helps the muscles, including the heart to relax. Sodium occurs naturally in foods therefore, most people don't have a problem getting enough sodium. Reduce your intake of foods such as chips, salted crackers, pretzels, popcorn and salted nuts or try the low-salt or unsalted version.

Also reduce your intake of pre-packaged foods, processed meats, canned foods and condiments which are loaded with salt. If you use the salt shaker, use it sparingly. Consuming too much sodium may be a contributing factor for hypertension. Research indicates there is a link between sodium and high blood pressure in people who are considered "salt sensitive." Make gradual changes to give your taste buds time to adapt to the change.

7. *Eat calcium-rich foods.* Calcium is a very important mineral in the diet. Make sure you include calcium-rich foods such as milk, cheese, yogurt, and cottage cheese. Try the low-fat versions. If you have problem consuming milk, choose lactose-free products. Getting sufficient calcium is important to prevent osteoporosis, which is a disease that causes brittleness and fractures in the bones due to calcium loss. Check the plant sources of calcium too. The following list can help you make healthier calcium selections:

- Switch from whole milk to low-fat or 1% milk.
- Try non-fat or low-fat versions of your favorite cheeses or use part-skim.
- Buy sliced cheese to control your portion sizes.
- Choose low-fat or skim buttermilk.
- If you drink rice milk, soy milk or other options try the low-fat version.

8. *Read food labels and check the serving size.* It is very important to know what you are eating. Food labels are your best source of information. From the label you'll learn how much fat, sodium, certain nutrients, cholesterol, fiber and other substances are in the food you buy. Once you start reading food labels you won't buy the same. This is a great way to know what is in the foods and will allow you to make better food choices.

You should read the ingredients to know what you're getting. The label tells whether the food is made from a natural grain like "whole" wheat or artificial ingredients or a grain that has been stripped of its nutrients and fiber. One of the first values listed on a nutrition label is the number of calories. Another important value is the serving size. This is the item you have to pay close attention to. You may read a label that says an item has 150 calories. You may think it's referring to the whole bag of cookies or chips. But the calories listed are "per serving size". Then you realize that a serving size may be only three cookies. If you eat six small cookies you need to double the calories, the fat, the sugar and all the other values. So check out the serving size listed on a package to determine what the calories and nutrients really mean to you and your health.

It's also important to read the label to find out the ingredients. They are listed in order, with the first being the ingredient present in the greatest amount and the last being present in the least amount. Look for foods that list more wholesome natural products first. Also, beware of foods listing a lot of artificial ingredients. If you can't recognize it or pronounce it, how natural can it be?

A summary of food labels:

- List ingredients from the greatest to the least amount
- Provide calories and the nutritional content of foods (such as vitamins, minerals, fiber, sodium, fats, carbohydrates, and sugars)
- Provide serving sizes for food comparisons
- Help you make better food choices
- Help you identify foods that contain artificial ingredients
- Help you know what you're putting in your body

9. *Limit your intake of fast foods.* Many foods at fast food restaurants are loaded with fats, oils, sugars and artificial ingredients. In addition, many of the foods have no real nutritional value for good health. These foods should not be consumed frequently. They are loaded with calories and one meal at a fast food restaurant can

have all of the required calories for the entire day. Some fast food restaurants now have healthier alternatives on their menu. And don't fall for the two-for-one sale. It's not a real savings if it gives you twice the calories and leads to illness. It's only a deal if you're going to share one meal or take another one home.

10. *Make better selections at restaurants*. Choose better food choices at restaurants. Ask for your dressing on the side, which allows you to control the amount you put on your salad. One table spoon of dressing contain 120 calories, which defeats the purpose of getting a salad. Most portion sizes are large at restaurants, so ask for a box to go to avoid overeating and you'll also have a meal for later.

11. *Eat smaller, frequent meals throughout the day*. The amount of meals you eat per day is important. Eating at least three meals per day and snacks in-between or four to six smaller meals spaced out evenly over the course of the day is best. This allows your blood sugar level to remain constant throughout the day so you function with a good energy level. It prevents you from crashing or feeling so hungry that your become weak, irritable, unable to concentrate, or get a headache and then eat uncontrollably later.

Eating smaller frequent meals helps you avoid bingeing or eating out of control by not going too long without eating. Have you ever gone the entire day without eating and once you get home in the evening and take the first bite, you can't stop eating until you fall asleep? Eating small frequent meals prevents a ravaging appetite and also keeps your metabolism steady. Smaller lighter frequent meals will also prevent fatigue and sluggishness that often follows eating a heavy meal.

Eating smaller frequent meals actually improves your metabolism and keeps you from overeating and stretching out your stomach. When you skip meals your metabolism decreases as your body protects itself from possible starvation. The body was programmed to do this. In my past I would go all day without eating and thought I was doing great. By the time evening came, I was so hungry I ate whatever I could grab until I was so stuffed I felt intoxicated. Then I went to sleep on all those extra calories. The next morning I was too full to eat breakfast and this cycle--skipping breakfast and overeating in the evening—continued. In the process I actually gained weight.

Please don't skip breakfast. This is the most important meal, as your body needs food to recover from its nighttime fast. In the long run skipping meals affects all areas of your life, including your job. Some people say they cannot eat breakfast. What I discovered over the years is that many people cannot eat breakfast because they eat so heavy at night. If you don't overeat at night and don't eat at least two hours before bedtime, you will appreciate breakfast in the morning. If you still don't have much of an appetite for breakfast, at least eat something light like a yogurt, fruit like a banana or a fruit smoothie.

12. *Avoid eating late at night.* There are many people who avoid eating during the day and then find themselves eating uncontrollably at night. It's very important to start out your day with breakfast and eat small meals throughout the day to avoid overeating at night. During the day is when you are the most active and need the majority of your calories. You slow down in the evening. So when you eat at night, if you have not burned sufficient calories during the day, you will go to sleep on those extra calories. Late night eating can contribute to weight gain.

In addition, eating late can cause you to wake up feeling groggy and sluggish, as your body had to work all night to digest all of the calories. Try to avoid eating no later than two hours before you go to bed and even that shouldn't be a heavy meal. When you go to bed at night you shouldn't feel stuffed. You also shouldn't be hungry. You should feel like you could eat a little if you wanted to, but the truth is you're just fine.

13. *Plan meals ahead*. In this day and time we live in, meal planning is crucial. We plan for our weddings, vacations, leave from work, holidays and other events and activities. Yet when it comes to an area as important as our health we tend to neglect this area. The food we eat is critical to our overall well-being. If we are not eating healthy we won't be able to enjoy the other events and activities in our lives. We won't be as productive at work, at home, in church and in the community. Although we have hectic schedules, we must set aside the time for meal planning. It's a good idea to plan meals in advance before you go to the grocery store and take a grocery list with you so you won't get off track. If you really find you don't have the time to cook daily, cook enough at one meal to last for two to three days.

14. *Listen to your body*. Have you eaten until you were so full you had to unbutton your pants or felt like you had to take a nap? Your body was trying to tell you something. Long before people counted calories and read food labels, there was a simple way to determine whether you needed to eat or had eaten too much. It was to listen to your body. When God created the human body, He created it with internal signals. When was the last time you felt hunger pangs or heard your stomach grumble? Have you heard your stomach frequently? We are so inundated with food in our society we no longer listen for our body to signal us for hunger. Food is everywhere and we tend to eat out of habit or just because it's there.

There is no way to escape food, the smell of it or the constant reminders. Even when we aren't genuinely hungry we eat for the taste, out of boredom, to socialize or for some other reasons. But it's time to stop and listen to your body. Allow your body to feel the hunger again. Don't eat so much during the day that you can never feel a hunger pang signaling you that it's time to eat. If you are not hungry, don't eat just because the food is there.

Plus your body will let you know when you are full. Many times we eat so fast, by the time we realize we are full, we've already eaten the whole thing. It's time to slow down, drink water during meals and in-between bites and let you stomach tell you you've had enough. You shouldn't feel stuffed after a meal or have your stomach poke out so far you have to unbutton your pants. You should feel just satisfied. I've seen people unbuckle their pants after they eat or intentionally wear elastic pants to give them extra room when they go out and eat. We don't have to know anything about nutrition or eating right to recognize when we are hungry, when we are full or when we have eaten too much.

15. *Slow down and enjoy your food.* Eating too fast is a sure way to overeat. It takes about twenty minutes for the brain to get the message that you have eaten. If you eat your meal faster than that, you are overeating. You will continue to feel hungry because your body hasn't gotten the message that you have already eaten. Slow down and chew thoroughly. God gave us taste buds to enjoy every bite.

Frequently, we overeat because we really enjoy the taste of the food. But we eat so fast we have to go for seconds and thirds to really get a taste of the food we are eating. I don't think anyone will take the food off your plate. Drink water in between bites and enjoy your meal. Let the taste marinade in your mouth.

Take your time at work so you can enjoy your lunch. Many of us have short lunch breaks and we run out and buy food and then have 10 to 15 minutes left to eat. It requires planning to have sufficient time to eat. Don't eat while you're working, talking on the phone, watching television or doing something else. The other activities will distract you and you will easily overeat. Plus the distraction will hinder you from enjoying your food. You will want more because you missed it. I know we have all done it.

Make it a habit to take a couple of very small breaks at work to eat a light snack like a piece of fruit, trail mix or nuts or some other healthy choice. This will prevent you from overeating later when you get home. It will also improve your work performance by keeping you energized without feeling sluggish from large, heavy meals or fatigued from going too long without food in between meals. Your supervisor should appreciate you taking care of your health, which will improve your overall mood, productivity, energy level and work performance. In the long run it will decrease job absenteeism by reducing the risk of illnesses. There are employees who take cigarette breaks, which are detrimental to their health. Managers and supervisors should support a healthy snack break to keep employees functioning at their best.

In addition to practicing good eating habits, it is important to recognize temptations to develop a plan to overcome them. The following tips below are suggestions to help you overcome temptations when aiming to eat right:

1. Don't deprive yourself of all your favorite foods. They can fit into a healthy diet when eaten in moderation.
2. Choose a day of the week when you allow yourself to eat some of your favorites.
3. Avoid the foods you know you don't have any control over.
4. Don't bring certain foods home, if you know you will eat it all.
5. Buy small sizes, not the extra-value bags or packs.
6. Recognize those people and places that influence you to overeat.
7. Deal with the emotional triggers that cause you to overeat.
8. Find a hobby or something productive to do.
9. Get out of the dieter's mind frame.
10. Don't give up when you feel you've slipped up.
11. Don't skip meals.
12. Pray before you eat, take your time and enjoy every bite.

Step # 6 Activities:
A. *Answer the Following Questions:*

1. Why is it important to eat a variety of foods?

2. What is the most important nutrient for your body? Why?

3. Why are natural foods important for the body?

4. What is the best way to ensure you're getting a sufficient amount of nutrients?

5. Why is it more important to eat food for nutrients rather than taking supplements only?

6. What are the six essential nutrients for the body?

7. Why is fiber important for the body?

8. Name some foods rich in fiber.

9. What can be a consequence of inadequate calcium in the body?

10. What is one of the best ways to know what's in the food you buy?

B. Check your frequency of consuming natural foods. Keeping a journal is a great way to keep track of what you eat. Also writing out your feelings and emotions is a great stress relief to avoid emotional eating.

    1. How many fruits and vegetables do you eat per day?

    2. How often do you eat whole grains?

    3. What is your plan to eat more fruits and vegetables?

    4. What is your plan to drink enough water?

    5. Name 2-3 small changes you can make to improve your eating habits.

Examples:

1. Add fruit with breakfast in the morning and mixed vegetables for dinner.
2. Cut back on frying meats.
3. Replace high-calorie snacks at night with fruit for dessert.

C. *Matching: Choose the best answers from the list below (answers can be used more than once:*

___1. Enhances the immune system	a. Whole grains
___2. Helps with vision	b. Fiber
___3. Strengthens bones and teeth	c. Carbohydrates
___4. Prevents anemia	d. Grains
___5. Prevents osteoporosis	e. Water
___6. Is linked to heart disease	f. Vitamin C
___7. The body's main energy source	g. Vitamin A
___8. Reduces risk of colon cancer	h. Calcium
___9. Nature's fast food	i. Protein
___10. Refreshes the atmosphere	j. Saturated fats
___11. The most important nutrient	k. Fruits
___12. Building material for body	l. Beans
___13. Found in meat and dairy	m. Vitamin D
___14. Insulation for the body	n. Iron
___15. Helps retention of calcium	o. Fat
___16. Rich in Vitamin C	
___17. Plant source of protein	
___18. Has nine calories per gram	
___19. Comes from the seeds of grasses	
___20. Sustainer of all life forms	

Answers to Section A: 1) to ensure you're getting an adequate supply of all the essential nutrients you need for good health 2) water/more than half of the body's weight is water and water is the most essential nutrient for life/waters satisfies thirst, carries nutrients throughout the body, enables a variety of chemical processes to take place, adds moisture to body tissues, softens stools, helps cushion your joints and aids in the regulation of body temperature 3) they contain vitamins, minerals, fiber, antioxidants and substances we don't know about yet for proper functioning of the body; they help with weight management because they are naturally low in fat; and they decrease the risk of disease and illnesses 4) eat a well-balanced diet that consists of a variety of foods 5) nutritionists believe that the nutrients are better absorbed by the body when eaten in the natural food and there are naturally occurring micronutrients in natural foods; when you eat the food you're getting the good stuff we know about and the stuff we don't know about yet 6) water, carbohydrates, protein, fat, vitamins and minerals 7) fiber decreases constipation, can reduce the risk of colon cancer, and even lowers blood cholesterol level; because fiber increases regularity, it can remove from the body more quickly the stool and toxins that can contribute to colon cancer 8) fruits, vegetables and whole grains are excellent sources of fiber 9) osteoporosis, which is a disease that can cause brittleness and fractures in the bones due to calcium loss 10) read the food labels and look at the ingredients from the greatest to lease amounts. *Answers to Section C* 1)f 2)g 3)h 4)n 5)h 6)j 7)c 8)b 9)k 10)e 11)e 12)i 13)j 14)o 15)m 16)k 17)l 18)o 19)a 20)e

STEP 7

FAITHFULLY WORKOUT

As the stomach was made for food, the body was made for God. He created our bodies to express the life He has given us and to fulfill our God-given purpose. Therefore, good health is true wealth to serve Him and others. But how can we help someone else to the best of our ability if we don't take care of ourselves? And how can we enjoy life to the fullest if we neglect our bodies? Faithfully working out is one of your best investments for a better quality of life.

Over the many years, we all have heard the many benefits of regular physical activity. People tend to associate exercise with its aesthetic benefits of improving the physical appearance. But exercise does a whole lot more than help you lose weight. If the benefits of exercise could be bottled, people all over the world would fight to own its rights. Yet it can be free and everyone do not take advantage of this life-changing activity.

The effects of exercise produce many physiological benefits within the body. These internal changes are manifested on the outside, which results in reshaping and transforming the body. One of the most important benefits of exercise is how it affects the heart. The heart is the most important and hardest working muscle in the body. Exercise makes both the heart and lungs more efficient and stronger. The improved blood circulation strengthens every life-sustaining organ and reduces the risk of stroke, cardiovascular disease, high blood pressure, diabetes and other illnesses. In addition, exercise improves the metabolic functions in the body. This helps the body burn more calories and increase lean muscle tissue. The result is losing body fat and gaining a shapelier firmer body. Exercise strengthens all muscles in the body and makes the whole body stronger to operate more efficiently.

Exercise has to become a lifestyle. Committing to a regular exercise regimen requires discipline and consistency for the best results. Yet, many people prefer quick fixes and fad diets to lose weight. Quick-fix diet plans take the weight off, but you are more likely to gain it back quickly. Not only that, quick fixes do not allow you to experience the physiological health benefits of exercise. Quick fixes focuses on reducing pounds. Regular exercise makes the whole body healthy and strong, from the inside out.

Exercise works for the body like faith works in our lives
Working our bodies reminds me of working our faith. We have faith in our paychecks paying our bills. We have faith in a promotion to get a new house or a newer car. We even place faith in our loved ones, coworkers, supervisors, or friends. Mark 11:22 says, *"Have faith in God."* Just think about it—without God none of these things or people would even exist. What if you don't get the promotion? What if your loved ones or friends let you down or they are not in a position to assist you? Well, a promotion, bank account, people or popularity do not dictate God's blessings. He can use whatever or whoever to bring His promises into fruition in our lives. When we have faith in God absolutely nothing will be impossible!

"Trust" and "faith" are often used synonymously, but they have different meanings. Faith is based more on one's belief. It can be defined as a firm belief or strong conviction in something for which there is no proof. When we have faith in God we can trust God, however, we believe Him for what we do not see. We believe God based on His character and the promises in His Word.

Exercising faith and faithfully working out have similarities. Both physical and spiritual exercise can be painful or uncomfortable. And you don't see immediate results. You have to work through the pain and discomfort believing your results will manifest in time. After starting a new exercise regimen, people tend to quit prematurely because of the pain, the work, or impatience. Spiritually, people want to give up when they don't see a change in their situation fast enough. But results for both starts within. With consistency, commitment, and time, you have to hold on and believe that your work is not in vain and you will achieve your goals.

According to the Bible, every human being has been given a measure of faith. Faith is a gift from God freely given to each of us based on His saving grace. In Matthew 17:20 Jesus speaks of faith as a mustard seed. In this passage He explains to His disciples that even a little bit of faith has great power when God is with us. A mustard seed, which is one of the tiniest seeds of all, under the right conditions, grows into a very large plant. Likewise, even a small "seed" of faith is sufficient for God to do great works in our lives. The power of God combined with a little faith will help us achieve great goals. Exercise has similar results. You don't have to train like an athlete or workout until you drop to gain the benefits of regular physical activity. Small changes can make a big difference in your overall health and help you gain amazing results.

James 2:17 says, *"Thus also faith by itself, if it does not have works, is dead."* To be effective, our faith has to be exercised. If someone professes faith, apart from actions, it is useless. Believing God requires getting up from where you are and acting like what He said is going to happen. Genuine faith cannot be demonstrated apart from the work. Like faith, exercise requires work. People frequently talk about wanting to lose weight and often do nothing about it or easily give up. They try diet after diet and program after program. Then they search for quick fixes to get the weight off. In order to lose weight and keep it off the healthy way, the right action is required. You have to stop making excuses, get up from where you and put action into practice.

You can start by believing God will help you achieve your goals. And then get to moving. In the beginning you can expect muscle soreness or pain a day or so after starting a new exercise program. It is a normal response as the muscles adapt to unusual exertion. The pain actually leads to strength and endurance. Spiritually, healing is a process. Physically, we must wait to see the results of the discomfort of exercising. But the more you exercise the less it hurts until the pain eventually subsides. In time, you become stronger and you gain endurance. Spiritually, the only way to get stronger is by going through the trials of life. When you push through the pain the less it hurts as your faith grows stronger in the Lord. Faith has the amazing benefit of reshaping your entire life and defining your future. Physical exercise reshapes your body and defines your total well-being.

No matter how spiritual we are, neglect of the body eventually leads to premature physical deterioration and illnesses. Some illnesses and conditions are beyond our control. But we have to take control of what we can. Then by faith, you have to do you part, and trust God with His part. But God will not come down from heaven, zap a magic wand, and make you lose the weight. You have to work towards the goal. You have to put forth some effort. You have to abide by God's natural law and expect to receive whatever you put out. You have to know and believe by faith that He can give you the guidance and the strength to get up and move your body. And like the best investments, when you work your body, your body will work for you. In the everyday hustle and bustle of our lives, we have to fight for our faith. We also have to fight to set aside time to exercise. But it is worth the sacrifice.

No matter where you are right now, believe by faith you will be healthy, and you will have the energy to invest in your health. Believe by faith you will overcome the weight loss battle and you will gain control over your eating habits. Believe by faith that you will overcome the emotional crises that trigger you to neglect your health. But like faith, don't trust in your own effort, will power, or another diet plan. Place your faith in God leading you and guiding you to what works for your body and personality. He created you. And He knows what's best for you.

Exercise does a whole lot more than help you look better
There are people who think the message of healthier living is only for people who are overweight or obese. Someone who is small or appears "normal" in size may feel the message of health is not for him or her. Many people have a misconception that someone who is small or thin doesn't need to practice healthy living. Being overweight is only *one* factor that can contribute to illnesses and diseases. Proper nutrition and exercise are needed for everyone's good health, regardless of body size.

I've seen slim people who have very little energy and cannot walk up several steps without gasping for air or are unable to perform daily activities with ease. Regardless of body size, everyone's hearts and lungs need activity for optimum performance. And small people's bodies still needs vital nutrients and plenty of water for proper functioning and disease prevention. All people need to be able to perform their everyday activities to the best of their ability.

Today, many people focus on the aesthetic benefit of exercise. But there are no short cuts to good health. All of the wonderful benefits of exercise extend way beyond the outside. And in order to gain these benefits, you have to put in the work. When we do what the body was created to do, wonderful things happen in our lives. The truth of the matter is, when I was younger I focused on the change in my outside appearance when I exercised. Now that I'm a lot older, I realize that committing to regular exercise does a whole lot more than help me look better. Exercise is critical for my total well-being.

Exercise improves so many physiological reactions in the body that it is impossible to name them all. Obviously, the body was created to be used by God and to operate a certain way. Can you imagine neglecting your car by not getting tune-ups, oil changes and other work done to keep it in good running condition? If you neglect proper maintenance of your car it will let you know. Eventually it won't start when you want it to. It will fail to run properly or it will break down altogether. The body needs proper maintenance as well. Scientists have discovered there are dramatic changes in our overall health when the body gets regular physical activity. The body was made to move.

Exercise not only helps with weight management and improves your posture. Regular physical activity improves so many more physiological functions in the body. As a quick review: Exercise improves your sleep and alleviates symptoms associated with anxiety, stress, PMS, menopause and depression. Exercise improves your concentration, boosts your self-image, and improves your mood and overall attitude. Exercise gives you more energy and stamina to perform your daily activities with ease. Exercise reduces body aches and pains, helps older people with balance and coordination, and helps you look younger longer. You'll think better, sleep better, concentrate better, feel so much better and yes, you will look better too.

Exercise can reverse or minimize existing health conditions such as high blood pressure, diabetes, and high cholesterol. Exercise is like a miracle cure for the body inside and out. Plus exercise is a natural remedy God gave mankind to help us deal with the many stresses and ills in life. When you don't set aside time for regular exercise, it is like a having a deadly disease and refusing the miracle cure. Exercising today can save you a whole lot of money on prescriptions, doctor visits, and job absenteeism due to health problems later in life. No matter where you are, it is not too late to get started.

Stop making excuses and get up and move
The lack of physical activity or a sedentary lifestyle is a major culprit in the epidemic of obesity and diseases. Many people think that only people who are considered morbidly obese or 100 pounds overweight need to be concerned about the effect extra weight has on their health. But experts agree that losing as little as five to ten pounds can improve your overall health and energy level. Try walking around with five pound weights on each leg. Then notice how much lighter you feel when you remove them.

Plus it is time to stop blaming our weight gain on child bearing or getting older. These have some influence on our weight, but they are not the only culprits. It is a lifestyle problem. Then it is a choice. It is true that every ten years our metabolism, the rate at which the body burns calories, decreases. But if you really look at the whole picture you can probably admit that your lifestyle has also changed. Are you as active as you were when you were younger? The change in your metabolism should not be an excuse to accept extra weight gain. With this in mind, if you are in your thirties, forties or fifties and you are eating the same way you did in your teens or twenties, you are going to gain weight.

As we get older we also lose lean muscle tissue that helps burn more energy. Then we start storing fat in unwanted areas. And although someone could be at the same weight today that they were when they were younger, they will most likely have less muscle tissue and more fat on their body. When you were younger you were more active. As we age, we have to make a conscious effort to watch our weight by incorporating physical activity into our daily lifestyle. The reality is, many Americans fail to meet the minimal exercise requirements for good health or to maintain a healthy weight.

Then our lifestyle has changed drastically from the past. Years ago, if you wanted to eat, you grew your own food and then worked to gather it and prepare it. People ate natural foods from the earth and were naturally active to survive. Today, many people sit at computers most of the day. We don't have to get up to change the television station. Even our children play video games, watch television, sit at computers, and get very little physical activity at home or in school. Poor food choices combined with the lack of activity have created the perfect storm for extra pounds and bad health.

Your body is the only vehicle or instrument you have to express your existence on this earth. And you are God's investment to reveal His riches in the lives of others. But unlike cars, we only get one body. So we should to do our best to take care of the one we've got. Plus life is a precious gift. It's time to stop making excuses and let your body work for you. And when you are good to your body, your body will be good to you. You will be able to accomplish so much more in your life and the lives of others, with more energy and the right attitude.

The recommendation of exercising for good health

So how much exercise is enough? Major health organizations have recommended that all Americans accumulate at least thirty to sixty minutes of moderate-intensity physical activity, preferably most days of the week. The recommendation for children and teenagers is to be physically active for 60 minutes most days of the week. So how can you get started? Walking is fun, safe, effective and it's free. You can start a waking group on your job, in your community, or at church. Remember that the right action is required to achieve weight loss goals. Find your balance between food and your activity. If you are physically active for at least 30 minutes several times a week, you can have amazing results.

Be aware: One of the biggest mistakes beginners make is exercising too hard, for too long, or too frequently. In fact, moderate intensity gets the best results for weight loss. If you are beginning to walk, ride a bike or some other activity, start out slowly. Don't overwork. You should be able to exercise and still talk and not be out of breath. If your goal is to walk three days a week and you can only do 10-15 minutes a day starting out, that's great. You have time to work up to more time and more days. Some people join the gym and work out so hard and so frequently that they get frustrated and burn out. They fall by the wayside and stop working out altogether. This has been an ongoing episode in health and fitness centers across the country; especially when people make their New Year's resolution.

People also make the mistake of focusing on their body weight, rather than making healthy living a part of their everyday regimen.

When healthy living becomes part of your lifestyle, weight loss is inevitable. Again, strive to be fit and the look with be your tip. Strive to work out three to five days a week and exercise a minimum of 15 minutes at a time, gradually increasing your time as you get in better shape. You may experience some mild or slight discomfort when you start a new activity. Before long the soreness will subside as your body adapts to its new workload.

And listen to your body. Exercise should not be painful. "No pain, no gain" is a fitness fallacy. Mild discomfort can be expected. But if you are in pain, your body is telling you something is wrong. You need to stop. And if you experience any pain or pressure in the middle of your chest; dizziness, lightheadedness, or loss of coordination; or an abnormal heart reaction you should stop immediately and consult your physician. Before beginning any new exercise program you should consult your doctor.

Before you exercise, begin with a warm-up by performing a low-intensity exercise. This gradually prepares your body for greater movement. For instance, if you're going jogging around a track, walk a lap or two first. The gradual increase in exercise intensity allows adequate blood flow to the heart and muscles to prevent damaging them. Include static stretching to increase flexibility or improved range of motion, allowing you to move more freely. Do not bounce while stretching as this can cause injury to the muscles.

If you are going to swim, instead of focusing on the lower body, stretch the upper body (arms, shoulders, back, and chest). Stretching should also be done after exercising. A warm-up prepares the body for the activity; stretching before and after activity helps improve range of motion and prevent injuries. Then make sure you include a cool down period to prepare the body to decrease the activity before you actually stop. A cool down's major purpose is to prevent a major drop in arterial blood pressure, which can cause an insufficient supply of blood to reach the brain and cause dizziness, light-headedness, and even fainting.

Both aerobic and weight resistance exercises are important for maximum health benefits. Aerobic exercise is any activity that uses the large muscle groups in the body. It is rhythmic in nature and can be performed or maintained continuously for a prolonged period of time. The cardiovascular and respiratory systems (the heart and lungs) play a major role in aerobic activity. One of the major benefits of aerobic activities is the improvement of the ability of the cardiovascular system to deliver oxygen to the body. Aerobic exercise makes the heart stronger, helps the body burn fat and results in an improved body image and better quality of life.

Examples of aerobic exercise include walking, jogging, running, cycling, aerobics, rowing, biking, cross-country skiing, hiking, inline skating, and rollerblading. You can purchase equipment or go to a fitness center and use equipment that provides aerobic exercise. This includes equipment such as a treadmill, stationary cycle, elliptical, rowing machine, or stair climber.

In addition to aerobic exercise, weight resistance activities are important. They increase lean body mass, decrease the risk of bone loss, and increase metabolism. Strength training is important because of the subsequent improvement of the musculoskeletal system. Weight resistance exercise helps with weight management by helping to maintain and build muscle tissue. More muscle tissue helps you burn fat faster and helps you develop a tone, stronger, shapelier body. The recommendation is at least two days per week to help you perform the activities of everyday life with ease and decrease the risk of injury. Weight resistance activities include working out with weights or weight resistance bands or tubes at home or in the gym. Some people are creative at home using books, pans, and soup cans as weights to strengthen their muscles.

There are many exercises claiming to be "the one" to get you in shape. Whatever you do, find something you enjoy, so you are more likely to stick to it. If you do not enjoy the activity, it will probably soon become work and you will find yourself in a slump again. Or like I often do, use your exercise time as a time of worship so that an otherwise boring activity can be uplifting and exciting. I also use it as my bonding time with the kids. I put on my favorite inspirational music and we walk, dance and step to our hearts' content. In addition, there are a variety of group exercise classes available at fitness centers, recreation centers, churches, exercise studios and other organizations. There are so many choices and there may also be some activities you never considered to get you up and moving. Find what works for you and get moving.

Always remember to start out slowly. Choose a variety of activities and set aside a specific time to exercise. Then stick to it like any other important appointment. Research concludes inactivity is one of the major contributing factors for so many diseases. Many factors can contribute to excessive weight, yet nutritionists, health experts and scientists all agree that the primary cause is an imbalance between calorie consumption and caloric expenditure. Basically, taking in too much energy and not expending or using enough energy through activity is a big problem. Three to five days of cardiovascular activities and two days of resistance training is a recommendation for good physical health.

In addition to sticking to a regular workout schedule, here are other ways to incorporate regular activity into your daily life:

1. Walk up the stairs instead of using the elevator or escalator.
2. Park your car at the far end of the parking lot and walk briskly to your destination.
3. Put on some of your favorite energizing music and clean your house with gusto.

4. If you sit at a computer most of the day, get up and take five-minute breaks, stretching and walking.
5. Walk your dog; walk around your neighborhood or to the park with family members after dinner.
6. Walk around your building during part of your lunch break; walk around the mall, or start a walking group on your job, in your church, or in the community.
7. Wash your car, mow your lawn, or do some gardening with gusto.
8. Play actively with your kids or grandkids. Jump rope, play kickball, volleyball, skate, go bowling or other fun activities. Or just dance or run around the house or yard with the kids.
9. When you have to use the restroom at work, walk to one farther away from your office.
10. Put on your favorite music and just move. Do jumping jacks, jog in place, and step side to side. Just have a great time moving it to use it.
11. Go to bed earlier. Exercise first thing in the morning to get it out of the way.
12. Exercise during your lunch break at work or right after work to reenergize.
13. Schedule exercise and stick to it like any other important appointment.
14. Get a fitness partner for support.
15. Get a personal trainer to help you reach your goals.
16. Join a health and fitness center.
17. Take group exercise classes.
18. Train to walk or run a marathon for a cure.
19. Purchase exercise equipment to use at home for convenience.
20. Walk on the treadmill or ride a stationary bike while watching TV or talking on the phone.

The following list is a review of exercise tips for success:

1. If you have chronic health problems, heart disease, or have been sedentary for a long time see your doctor and have a health screening before starting any exercise program.
2. One of the biggest mistakes beginners make is exercising too hard, for too long, or too frequently. In fact, moderate intensity gets the best results for weight loss. Don't overwork. Start our slowly. If you can only do 10-15 minutes a day, that's okay. Gradually increase your time and duration as you get in better shape. Eventually your goal should be 30 to 60 minutes of moderate activities most days of the week.
3. Aerobic exercise is extremely important for good health. Include at least three to five days of aerobic exercise a week.
4. Include weight resistance activities. Resistance training should be done at least twice a week.
5. Choose activities that are fun so you can to stick with it. Add a variety of activities to switch up on different days to avoid boredom.
6. Wear loose-fitting or comfortable clothing and dress appropriately for the weather and the activities. Proper footwear is also important for specific activities.
7. Listen to your body. If it hurts don't do it. Pain is a warning sign that something is wrong. However, when your first start an exercise program or a new routine, discomfort is normal until your body adapts to your new workout regimen.
8. Surround yourself with positive and supportive people. The reality is your environment and people can influence your behavior. Find people with similar goals of caring for their health to encourage one another.
9. Set realistic fitness goals and accomplish them before you move on to the next goal.

10. Keep a fitness journal to track your progress. And reward yourself for successes.
11. Do not become preoccupied with the scale. People often make the mistake of focusing on their body weight, rather than making healthy living a part of their everyday regimen. When you first start exercising, you will notice a change in your measurements and the way your clothes fit before you notice a change in the scale. Exercising increases muscle tissue and burns fat. Keep in mind that muscle weighs more than fat. It is not just about your weight, but your lean muscle and body fat ratio affects your overall health. You can always request a body fat test from a fitness trainer or fitness facility.
12. Be patient and don't give up. Many people quit because they don't see results fast enough. Allow exercise to become a part of your lifestyle. If you do, the results are inevitable. Remember, "Strive to be fit and the look with be your tip".
13. Before you exercise, begin with a warm-up by performing a low-intensity exercise to gradually prepare the body for greater movement.
14. Include static stretching to increase flexibility or improved range of motion, allowing you to move more freely.
15. Include a cool down period to prepare the body to decrease the activity before you actually stop.

The following list is only some of the many amazing benefits of exercise:

1. *Exercise improves the condition of your heart and lungs*. The heart is the most important muscle in the body because it pumps oxygen-rich blood and nutrients to every cell in the body. Exercise makes both the heart and lungs more efficient and

stronger. The heart has to work less when it operates efficiently, thus placing less stress on this life-sustaining organ. For instance, one of the reasons people are not able to walk up a flight of stairs without breathing hard is that the body is trying to consume more oxygen. So the heart has to pump harder. People who exercise regularly can walk up the stairs and perform other daily activities without becoming short of breath. Their hearts have to work less than that of the person who does not exercise. And because their hearts have to work less, they also generally have lower blood pressure and pulse rates. Physical fitness allows you to perform daily activities with greater ease.

2. *Exercise reduces the risk of various illnesses and diseases.* Research has shown that regular physical activity can decrease the risk of adult on-set diabetes, hypertension, heart disease, and certain types of cancers. It can lower blood cholesterol levels and decrease the risk of other illnesses associated with sedentary lifestyles. According to research, most of the illnesses we see today can be prevented by healthy lifestyle changes.

3. *Exercise increases muscular strength.* Physical activity such as weightlifting or muscle toning increases muscle fiber, making muscles stronger, thus increasing the body's ability to do work with greater ease. You are able to carry groceries, lift a small child, or move other items with less effort.

4. *Exercise improves muscular endurance.* You have more stamina and do not tire as easily.

5. *Exercise helps you lose weight.* Exercise helps you burn extra calories and unwanted pounds through the exertion of energy. When you burn more energy than you consume, you lose weight.

6. *Exercise increases your metabolism.* Increase in metabolism means that you burn calories or energy at a higher rate or quicker than someone who does not exercise. Someone

with a higher metabolism can eat more than someone the same size without gaining weight. Your body will burn fat even when you are not exercising or while you sleep.

7. *Exercise improves your body image*. By burning unwanted fat and increasing muscle tone, exercise improves your physical appearance and creates a slimmer, shapelier, firmer and healthier looking body. Being able to overcome obstacles and commit to healthy living improves your confidence. You're able to take charge of your life and work towards looking better, feeling better and having a better outlook on life.

8. *Exercise increases and maintains lean body mass*. One of the problems with weight loss programs is that you lose lean mass or muscle tissue while you are trying to lose unwanted fat. Exercising on a weight loss or weight management program helps you maintain and build lean muscle tissue, which is responsible for a healthy, fit body. Muscle burns more calories than fat because it requires more energy to be maintained. Keep in mind fad diets are to be avoided because they break down lean muscle tissue.

9. *Exercise improves your posture*. When the muscles are stronger and firmer, the body is erect rather than slouched over or out of alignment. Improved posture and stronger muscles also decrease the risk of lower back pain, a common ailment as we age.

10. *Exercise increases bone strength*. Weight-bearing activities such as running, walking, and weightlifting strengthen the bones, which decreases the risk of osteoporosis, a condition that causes fractures and brittleness of the bones. Exercise helps older people avoid crippling falls where these fractures can occur.

11. *Exercise reduces depression, stress, and anxiety*. Doctors prescribe regular physical activity for depression because it is a natural antidepressant and tranquilizer. Exercise also

relieves stress and anxiety that may be associated with the many pressures we face in life. Endorphins or hormones released during exercise have a very calming effect. God gave us a natural tranquiller!

12. *Exercise reduces symptoms associated with PMS and menopause.* Again, the hormones released during exercise make physical activity an alternative drug therapy for some women who suffer with various mood swings, pain, irritability, and other physical and emotional symptoms associated with these conditions, including premenopausal symptoms.

13. *Exercise improves your mood.* Exercise relieves tension and make you feel more confident, which results in a more positive attitude. It also improves your concentration and helps you to focus.

14. *Exercise helps you keep off the weight.* Studies show that most people who diet gain the weight back within the first year. But those who remain physically active are the most successful at keeping the weight off.

15. *Exercise helps you eat less.* Some people think if they start exercising they will have a tremendous appetite. But exercise can actually suppress the appetite. This is true for me. I ate due to stress and anxiety. Exercise helped relieve some of these feelings, therefore, I snacked a lot less. Exercise also seems to create a healthy mind-set. You want to eat less unhealthy foods and tend to make healthier food choices. Regular exercise may actually decrease cravings for unhealthy choices.

16. *Exercise reduces medical expenses.* People who exercise regularly and take care of their health tend to be ill less often than those who don't exercise at all.

17. *Exercise reduces job absenteeism and improve job performance.* People who take care of their health and exercise are absent from their jobs less frequently due to fewer illnesses.

Job performance improves because of the benefits exercising has on the body and mind.

18. *Exercise helps you sleep better.* Exercise relaxes the body and mind, which helps you go to sleep easier and sleep well. It helps you enjoy a better quality of rest.

19. *Exercise improves athletic performance.* Physical activity improves your cardiovascular capacity, muscular strength, and endurance for improved performance in various sports activities.

20. *Exercise improves the overall quality of your life.* I'm not going to tell you that if you exercise you will definitely live longer. But I know for sure that you will feel a whole lot better while you're living. Research shows that exercise allows you to feel younger longer by preventing premature aging. Regardless of how long you live, taking care of your health allows you to live a more energetic, healthier and productive life.

It's time to discover the joy in fitness and get up and move! Exercise is truly one of the best methods of healing available to us. Combined with prayer and faith, taking care of your body is one of the best things you can do to continue the journey of total health.

Get proper rest to refresh your body, soul and spirit

Keep in mind, if you start a new exercise program, a new job or any new routine requiring more effort, you will need more rest. In the beginning your body needs more recovery time for its new workload. Once you become better physically conditioned or your body adapts to the new activity, it requires less recovery time and you will need less sleep. God didn't make any mistakes. He created a twenty-four hour day and a human body that can get sufficient rest in that time period.

In the hustle and bustle of our everyday lives, we get so caught up in the everyday affairs of living. Then we neglect a basic need for rest for recovery of the body, mind and spirit. Our bodies are not like computers or machines that we turn on and keep running until we decide to turn them off. The human body will break down without sufficient rest. It will manifest through irritability, anxiety, stress, the inability to concentrate, frustration, illnesses, or even depression. Various health problems are associated with fatigue and overwork.

In addition to eating right and exercising, we have to remember that sufficient sleep is crucial for our overall health. The lack of sleep inadvertently affects your immune system making you more susceptible to illnesses and affects your body's ability to protect itself and to heal and recover during an illness. At times, we will push past our body's limit and get less sleep for certain events or to accomplish certain goals. But doing this regularly causes more harm than good for our overall well-being.

When it comes to getting sufficient rest, it is important to be as consistent as possible with your sleep schedule. Strive to go to bed around the same time each night and try to get the same amount of sleep per night. The lack of sufficient rest is a sure way to escalate stress. The lack of rest also makes you forgetful and affects your short-term memory. Proper rest helps you to concentrate and to focus, and to make sound decisions, especially during stressful times.

The amount of sleep you need varies depending on what's going on in your life. However the recommended estimate is eight hours per night, which varies from person to person. How do you feel when you wake up in the morning? Do you feel refreshed and energized ready to start the new day? Or do you hit the snooze button several times? Also keep in mind that too much sleep is not better. It can make you tired and sluggish too.

In addition, get sufficient rest for your mind by taking the time to wind down. Take a break from all of your responsibilities. Soak in a nice warm bubble bath. Get a massage, pedicure or manicure. Go to the park and enjoy the atmosphere and scenery; and don't take any work with you. Meditate on God's wonderful creations as you look at the trees, the birds in the air, the beautiful blue sky and the clouds above. Take your children or grandchildren to a park or playground and run and play with them. Get on the sliding board, swing in the swing or enjoy the seesaw. Take your dog for a nice long walk and enjoy the scenery. Do something different and relaxing to break up the stress and monotony in your life.

Changing your environment can make a difference in the way you feel. Go to the movies. Discover a hobby. Discover what types of activities help you unwind. Commit to the time to take care of yourself and get proper rest. And don't forget to exercise and rest your spirit through regular prayer time and by reading God's Word's. Then you can be spiritually, emotionally and physically refreshed, restored and renewed to do all that God created you to do.

Step #7 Activity: Keep track of exercise

I. Record your daily activities in a journal and track your progression. You can use the example below:

Week of: _____

	Activity	Duration
Monday:		
Tuesday:		

Wednesday:

Thursday:

Friday:

Saturday:

Sunday:

II. Answer the following questions:

1. Name several benefits of physical exercise.

2. What obstacles prevent you from committing to regular exercise?

3. How can you overcome these obstacles and commit to regular exercise?

4. How do you unwind or what can you do to take time for yourself?

5. Do you get sufficient rest? Why or why not?

6. How can you set aside the time to get sufficient rest?

7. Name some of your hobbies.

8. How can you improve your prayer life?

9. How can you spend more time reading God's Word?

10. How can you develop a plan to take better care of your total well-being?

STEP 8

GIVE IT THE
BEST YOU'VE GOT

The hater games show us that human frailties *will* fail you. Human beings emotional states are complicated. And you can be sure that they *will* change. People will take you on an emotional roller coaster ride, if you let them. They can be up one moment and down the next. They can praise you one week and criticize your short-comings the following. Or someone you thought liked you can tear you down to impress someone else. People's moods, attitudes and views determine how they treat you from day to day.

The hater games teach us that God is the only One we should exclusively trust. He never changes. And God will never fail you. He is always the same and His promises are unshakable. He is the *One* source you can always count on. Unlike our critics, when God reveals short-comings, it is only to make us better. His example inspires the best leaders to bring out the best in people for success in every area of life.

A hater's game is an eye-opening experience. It reveals underlying issues of the heart. This makes it easy to criticize our critics, right? But if we pause for a moment, as mentioned previously, we discover hidden issues within our hearts. Either way, the pain produces change. But we have a choice. We can allow the insults and criticism to negatively shape our thoughts and actions. Or we can learn to continuously grow on this journey of life.

One of the issues that hater games pushes to the surface of our hearts is pride. A hater's intent is to make you look bad in the eyes of others. And let's be real. We are deeply hurt by their criticism, insults and gossip. But the hurt is often our ego. Pride is an issue of the heart when we are more concerned about what people think about us, than what God thinks. And pride is definitely the problem when we feel we have something to prove to others.

To take it further, pride is the culprit when we rely on human effort or feel that we are self-sufficient. Pride is when we think we deserve more, instead of being grateful for what we have. Pride takes credit for gifts, talents, and accomplishments or connects to others because of their abilities or position. Obviously, there is nothing wrong with taking pleasure in our achievements and accomplishments. But it becomes pride when we take credit or give others credit for what God has done. Plus, when we think more highly of ourselves than we ought to or feel that we are better than others, we are dishonoring God with pride.

God alone gives men and women the ability to accomplish great goals. God gives people the ability to obtain a degree, income or lifestyle. The Bible says God opens doors that no one can close and He closes doors that no one can open. Our absolute best efforts to achieve our goals can only be accomplished *if* God allows us to succeed. He gives the wisdom, strength and knowledge to pursue our ambitions. He gives our intellectual ability, creativity, and innovative ideas. He chooses our genetic make-up from our parents for the attributes and characteristics to fulfill our purpose.

We cannot take credit for any good thing. The Bible says that every good and perfect gift comes from above. That means all that we have and all that we are belong to God, who is Maker of heaven and earth and the entire universe. Therefore, we don't have to prove anything to anyone. All human beings are in the same situation. We can only accomplish goals *if* God allows them to happen.

Humility defeats pride. Humility recognizes God's sovereign position to reign in our lives as our true source and provider. Humility recognizes that He is the One who is truly in control of all things. Humility recognizes without Him we can do nothing of ourselves. Humility is a reflection of thanks to God for all that we have and for all that we are.

During one of the hater games that inspired this message, I had to be honest with myself. It was painful that my performance was tainted. It bothered me that my hard work and efforts were not appreciated. And it deeply hurt that folks I encouraged spoke negatively about me. Some of my critics were younger or had a lot less experience which felt more insulting. I could not believe that grown folks would tattletale and bully others in a professional environment, like school-aged kids.

The daily scrutiny, fault-finding, and negativity was so discouraging. They try to make you feel like something is wrong with you or you start to doubt or question yourself. What made it worst was that my critics' negative perspectives influenced others. Those who believed the false accusations did not have the experience or knowledge to recognize the hater games. Or they were players on the team. At the time, I had no idea that I would unjustly endure such lowly places and situations. On top of that, I thought that my plans failed and I was extremely disappointed. At the time, I had no idea that God was using what I thought was a mess to create this message.

Throughout school and my career, I was an overachiever who received numerous accolades and awards. So these intense blows tried to injure my self-image, integrity and self-respect. Quite frankly, it felt humiliating. This is when hidden pride was revealed in my heart. I had to learn how to put pride to the side. Matter of fact, it was being crushed. I learned that no matter how hard I worked, if God did not open the door, it was not going to happen. And if I did not accomplish certain goals, it was not God's plan. Most importantly, I learned that God sees everything; so what He thinks is more important than anyone else's views. I had to learn to trust in His ability to guide me where He wanted me to be. I had to rely on His help to achieve what He wanted me to accomplish. And I had to let go of caring about what others think about me. It was not easy.

In addition, I learned that we can make plans, but we have to plan for God's plans. In His eyes, our character is more important than our accomplishments. Character is more important than our comfort. Gifts and talents can take you where you want to go. But character helps you strive when you arrive. Character helps you overcome the challenges and temptations that come with higher places. Today, I know that these painful experiences were preparation for the vision God placed in my heart many years ago. So I had to push through the pain of the negative views, lies and insults, and trust God's better plan to bring something good out of it.

Yes, it is natural to desire recognition and appreciation for our hard work and efforts. But when we do this, we risk facing rejection, disappointment and feelings of failure. It is impossible to please all people. And it is impossible to meet everyone's expectations. If you try to please people, you will die trying. Not only that, the Bible says that if we seek to please people, we cannot please God. Plus if you worry about what others think about you, you will be discouraged. And if you wait to be recognized by people, you may wait forever. We have to change our attitude to win at life. When our efforts are not appreciated by others, God appreciates our efforts. As long as we have the right attitude and motive, we are successful in His eyes.

I cannot stress this enough: **You cannot allow people's opinions to determine how you feel about yourself.** You cannot rely on people's opinions about you. People have skewed views, opinions and prejudices based on their experiences, background, upbringing and inner struggles. You have to accept the fact that everyone will not like you or appreciate you. Some will be jealous or feel threatened or intimidated by what they admire or desire about you. And your critics rather see you look inadequate so they can feel better about themselves. But when we put pride to the side, we can focus on the real prize.

Colossians 3:23-24 says, *"And whatever you do, do it heartily as to the Lord and not to men, knowing from the Lord you will receive the reward of your inheritance, for you serve the Lord Christ."* When we change our focus and work for God, we won't be consumed by a critic's views. So wherever you are, give "it" the best you've got. In God's eyes no job is too small or mediocre. No matter where you are, when you seek to please God, you will be enthusiastic, cheerful and grateful that He sees your efforts.

What is "it"? It is whatever you do in life. If you're a mother, give it the best you've got. If you're a wife, give it the best you've got. If you're a homemaker, teacher, cleaning person, nurse, doctor, manager, lawyer, secretary, receptionist, file clerk, mentor, prayer partner, minister, choir member, family member or friend, give *it* the best you've got. And if God put you in it, He will give you the strength to get through it. And do not despise your small beginnings. And if you feel overlooked, remember that God sees all that you do. And He will use every single detail and experience to prepare you for the next level to your destiny.

People judge your performance based on their expectations. But God is the only One who can accurately judge the condition of a person's heart. He knows when you are sincerely doing the best with what you've got. Plus He knows when people are bias, unfair, and misjudge you based on their opinions, prejudices, expectations, insecurities and inner struggles. When your best efforts are not appreciated by others, don't be discouraged. Do your best and trust God with the rest. He has a sure reward.

Plus giving God your best significantly reduces stress. People's views about you will change from time to time. Family members, acquaintances, coworkers, supervisors and other people will change depending on what's going on in their lives. But when you give God your best, you won't have the emotional distress that accompanies pleasing others. And you don't have to be intimidated or defensive. You will be free to work with unshakable joy, knowing that you are pleasing your heavenly Father. At the end of the day, what He thinks is more important than anything else. People would like to believe that they are in control of your life and future. But Scripture is clear: Promotions come from God alone. He is the only One who is truly in control of all things. But He will allow your hater to look like he or she is in control for a moment, so He can show up and show Himself strong on our behalf.

The greatest fight is your faith

With God on your side, you don't have to fight your critics. The greatest fight is your faith. As your opponents throw shots, you have to believe what God has for you is for you. You have to believe that He has your future, your career, your family, your finances, your reputation, your health and your entire life in His hands. You have to believe that God will perfect every single thing that concerns you. You have to believe that nothing they do will stand, with the Most High God as your Defense. Remember, where your mind goes your body naturally follows. Our thoughts hold the key that unlock our success or hold the chain that keeps us bound and in distress. And the best way to master our emotions and hold on to our faith is by knowing the promises in God's Word.

The Word promises that no weapon formed against you shall prosper. In other words, your critics will throw shots, but they will not accomplish the intended damage. We can use the Word of God like boxing gloves. But we should not use Bible bullying to intimidate our opponents. The Word guards our hearts and minds. God's Word gives us the confidence to block a hater's attacks. And if we get knocked down, it's only for a moment. The Word of God uplifts our spirit, so we won't stay down for the final count.

The Word changes our inner hearts. When our inner lives changes, our behavior and lifestyle will readily change. We cannot change people, but God's Word increases our faith to respond the right way. And yes, at times doing the right thing will feel so wrong. But we have to believe that God is going to work it out for good. Then we can reshape our thoughts to line up with His vision for our lives. Haters are not going anywhere. If we could physically knock one out, another one would quickly appear out of nowhere. But God's promises help us redirect our emotional energy. So let it go. Learn what areas in your life need improvement. Then use the emotional energy to whole-heartedly focus on pursuing the goals and dreams in your heart.

When you focus on fulfilling your God-given purpose to the best of your ability, you won't be distracted by the hater's shots.

When you whole-heartedly focus on God's vision for your life, you won't have time to worry about who doesn't like you or who's talking about you. And you recognize the hater for who he or she really is—a hurting soul crying to be made whole. Quite frankly, your opponent needs your prayers. At the end of the day, this battle is spiritual. The reality is the enemy of God uses people's weaknesses to discourage others. But we are still dealing with precious souls. And it is not God's will for any soul to be lost. He wants to give everyone an opportunity to turn their lives over to Him.

Haters reveal greatness that you never knew was inside of you
God's passion is people. When someone tears down, disrespects and discourages people they are directly opposing God. God created human beings to be uplifted, loved and cherished. He never condemns us. He created us to get better as we grow in Him. There are so many biblical stories of how difficult people could not stop God's plans for His people.

David's story is another example. King Saul loved David, but when jealousy burned in his heart, he despised David. He hunted David like a wild animal and tried to kill him several times. But when David had the opportunity to kill Saul, he did not take matters in his own hands. He trusted God as Judge and his Defense. And at the appointed time, God kept His promise. What Saul meant for harm, God turned around for good. Saul had a horrible end and David became the king of the land. Today, we see many haters rise to the top or climb the corporate ladder by stepping on others. But with each step they take, that's how much lower they will have to fall one day.

Like King David, you don't have to retaliate. The Bible says without faith it is impossible to please God. Hold on to your faith. God wants you to stand strong and trust Him. This is not your battle.

The battle is the Lord's and it has already been won. Plus when we face opposition, we should get ready to celebrate. Opposition is an opportunity to see God at His very best. He specializes in turning around what seems so horrible for our good. David, Joseph, Esther and so many men and women of God placed their enemies in the hands of God. And God used the attacks to sharpen their character and prepare them for greatness.

Today, everyone is searching for greatness. But greatness is not a destination. We see many people reach high places as public successes. Then we later found out that the people we least expected struggled with private failures. Greatness is not based on outward appearance or achievements. The real place of greatness is the heart—having unshakeable trust, joy, hope, peace and faith in God. As we see in Joseph's, David's and Esther's stories, they reached high places they never imagined. But their sole purpose was to save the lives of nations. They experienced the "haters" of their time. Still today, haters will reveal greatness that you never knew was inside of you.

Hater games fuel the passion in your heart

God is so amazing that He has the divine ingenuity to use pain from the hater games to fuel our passion. Let's review passion for a moment. Passion has reciprocal qualities. Passion inspires us to achieve our goals, while empowering others to reach their full potential. Passion is often activated by personal pain and trials or by witnessing the mistreatment, struggles or injustice of others. Passion comes with a price. It is often the crises in our lives that reveal the passion in our hearts. The place of our greatest pain is often the place of our greatest passion. Life is full of challenges, disappointments and uncertainties that cause discouragement and doubt. So when you find your passion, hold on to it tightly and don't let it go.

As you pursue your passion pray for guidance. It is a good idea to get advice from an expert or someone who is where you want to be. Do not limit yourself to seeking the same opportunities as others or stick to one area or community. Be daring. Tap into diverse resources and arenas. Take the initiative to reach wider and higher. Get a broader perspective of the world to enhance your potential. Meet new people, discover new circles, attend events, or join organizations. Experience new cultures, learn a new language or travel abroad. Or at least visit beyond your city and state. Embrace diversity and accept people's differences. Expecting others to think like you or to be like you is a sign of limitations in your own life. If you really want change, *you* have to change. True passion takes you beyond your experiences, neighborhood, degree and upbringing. It allows you *to* put your best foot forward.

If God gave all of us gifts, have you ever wondered why some people are more effective using their gifts than others? Passion pushes you through the hurt of the hater games. Passion energizes you to perform in such a way that no trial, hardship or distraction can stop you. Passion helps you stay focused on your dreams and helps your gifts reach their full potential. When we rely on God's help, passion fuels success. Passion is the driving force to help you accomplish what God created you to do. As you whole-heartedly pursue your passion, your genuine enthusiasm and excitement for life will be contagious. And when your passion moves you, it will move others too.

Like the best investments, if your passion is going to work for you, you have to hang in there for the long run. So keep the vision before you. Write the vision down and describe what drives you to want to pursue it. Review it periodically. Then thank God for your critics. They help keep the fire alive and burning. Plus writing helps you release distress and discover solutions to overcome these games. In the book of Habakkuk, he asked God how long would it take for change to take place in the lives of God's people. God responded by telling Habakkuk to write down the vision and make it plain and it will come to past at the appointed time (Habakkuk 2:2-3). We don't wait any type of way. We wait with great expectation knowing that God is not like a human being who can lie or change His mind. God is faithful to keep all of His promises.

Writing down the dreams and goals God placed in your heart gives you hope as you patiently wait. It is a good idea to occasionally review what you have written during overwhelming times. Writing is a great mental boost by serving as a tool for emotional healing and as a reminder of what God has done and will continue to do in your life. Remember Joseph's haters wanted to kill his dreams. Don't let the dream killers discourage you. Tune out naysayers and doubters. Writing helps you to stay focused and keeps your dreams active and alive in your heart.

As you pursue your passion, take a good look at your inner circle and choose your friends and relationships wisely. Surround yourself with positive purpose-driven people who encourage you, help you grow and bring out the best in you. Avoid those who gossip, complain and tear others down. God loves us in spite of our imperfections. And He wants us to love others in spite of their faults and weaknesses. But we can choose to connect to people who desire to be healthy and whole and those moving in the same direction. And when you strive to give God your best, He will put people in your path to encourage you and support what He's placed on the inside of you. And He will surround you with favor to accomplish what He's created you to do.

And yes, God wants us to encourage and support those who are struggling; but not at the risk of damaging our lives. Scripture says that two are better than one. When one falls he can lift up his companion. On the other hand, bad company corrupts good character. As we grow in our relationship with God, He wants us to help others. But pray and ask Him to show you how to set boundaries to stay on the path of health and wholeness.

Life takes you through it, but God wants to use it
Physical exercise builds strong muscles and strengthens the most important muscle in the body, the heart. Working heartily for God strengthens our inner lives to live better on the outside. God wants to build you up and strengthen you for others. He wants us to conquer our inner lives to help someone else. How can you help others overcome difficulties, if you never had to endure? Life takes you through it, but God wants to use it. And a hater's game helps us learn how to break the hate. It gives us a heart of compassion to never want anyone to experience the pain of these games. We become more sensitive to how our words, attitude and actions affect others. In order to break the hate, we have to endure the hate. Not only that, in everything you do, someone is watching you. So don't give up, someone is counting on you for their breakthrough.

Breaking the hate includes breaking it from our younger generation. Older women should encourage younger women, not so much because they have a curvaceous figure, pretty face or wear the best outfits. The outside has its proper place. But why focus on their outside, when they are struggling to survive? Our younger generation are struggling with many challenges and temptations of these days and times. They need to know how to live better from inside out. They need to know how much God loves them to embrace loving themselves. They need to know that God will always be near to help them, guide them and He will never leave them alone. Our younger women need to know that each of them is uniquely made and beautiful in *His* sight. We should let younger women know that God *can* heal their broken hearts, give them a brand new start and He has a wonderful plan for their lives.

When we were younger, we were naturally self-centered and selfish and needed much healing. But as we become older, we should become wiser, stronger and better. We should be role models. We need to pray that discrimination and comparisons that lead to envy, jealously and unhealthy competition are broken. We can unite to break the hate that causes division, competition and insecurities. Some of these actions are learned behaviors that have been passed down to generations. Nevertheless, comparisons in appearances is part of a historical trauma that was used to conquer and divide. Therefore, we have to make a conscious decision to break the behavior which started with an original "hater".

And even if we made mistakes with our daughters or other women, we don't have to repeat the same mistakes. We can make a difference and start planting good seeds in the hearts of all women, including our daughters, granddaughters, nieces, sisters, friends and mentees. Especially if it was done to you as an adult or a child, why would you want someone else to feel the pain of rejection or of not feeling good enough? Somebody has to get in shape to break the hate! Why not you?

It is time to tear down the walls of our historical trauma that has divided generation after generation. Today, we are free to appreciate each other's differences. And if a woman is not able to build someone up; quite frankly, I believe she should keep her mouth shut. Still, it is not too late to change. If she sincerely focuses on becoming better, her latter days will be greater than her beginnings. God is able to heal us and deliver us at any age. To say "That's just the way I am or I have been like that all of my life", is denying the power of God.

There is absolutely nothing too hard for God. When we put our trust in Him, He can use us to make an incredible difference in the lives of others in our remaining years. And physical age does not necessarily indicate spiritual maturity. There is no age limit on who God can use. There are older woman who desperately need healing and change. And there are younger women who are making an amazing difference today.

The bottom line is we can never find a legitimate reason to tear down others, even when it is done to us. The Bible says that the enemy of God stands before Him night and day making accusations against God's children. Whether we want to accept it or not, the truth remains: This behavior is clearly influenced by the enemy of God. And I'll ask the questions again: Who is big enough to box with God? Who is bold enough to stand in His face and swing?

Be mindful: The enemy tries to use women's emotions to knock us out of the round. Or our emotions make us want to react and attack back. We can easily be taken by surprise and get so caught up in the emotional drama if we are not careful. Please remember, it is only a distraction to stop you from focusing on the great plans God has for your life. When you focus on what God has called you to do, you won't have time to think about what others are trying to do to you.

Turn it over to God and birth something wonderful
God has great plans, ideas, creativity and wonderful works for all of His precious women. But the enemy tries to use our emotions to keep us bound and in distress. But we *can* refuse to play the hater games. We can focus on the good and choose to be the best God created us to be. Like the human body has different parts to function effectively, we were created to work together. Each of us has an important role. There is no need to see another women as a threat

or competition. All of us are part of God's greater plan. We deceive ourselves when we think more highly of ourselves than we ought to. We all have different personalities, experiences, backgrounds, gifts and talents to reach different people. God wants to use all of His women to reach somebody somewhere. And He wants all of us in our proper positions.

We cannot choose our calling. It is God's prerogative how He chooses to use us. But we can choose how we respond to the hater games. We can choose to use the emotional energy for something good. For when you turn it over to God, you can birth something wonderful. My last hater's experience ignited a passion in my heart. And a place of great disappointment became a greater place of opportunity. I refused to retaliate and become a hater's player. My pain became a weighted gift to make me stronger and my travail led to the birth of this message. Now, I am more determined than ever to empower all women to unite and live life to the absolute fullest. And the pain of this treacherous game fueled my passion to take action to break the hate.

In addition, other changes took place in my heart. One of the most important differences in my life is experiencing God's freedom. I'm free from seeking to please others and I strive to please God in every area of my life. I'm free from worrying about what others think about me. What God thinks is more important than anything. So thank God I'm free from myself, free from others, free from my past and free from other people's views of success. True success is not found in materialistic possessions, money, titles, accomplishments, popularity, degrees or positions. People often look for an outward breakthrough. The greatest riches are treasures of the heart.

Today, I am so thankful for God's continuous flow of love, peace, joy, healing and hope that inspires me to enjoy the true meaning of life. My passion is to encourage people of all walks of life to pursue wholeness. God did it for me! And I want to share His amazing goodness, love, healing and freedom with people everywhere. Now I know that there is no limit to what I can achieve, even as a woman in my mid-fifties. Recently, I drove back to town with my dog and my clothes in my car. But I have Christ, and He is more than enough to start all over again.

Wherever you are, it is not too late! Wherever you've been, God will give you another chance. Refuse to listen to the lies of the enemy. God still has wonderful plans for all of His precious women. God can restore your youth and renew your energy and enthusiasm for life. When you give Him your best, He will revive your total wellbeing to make the best of the rest of your life.

God wants to use His precious women for His service
By teaching women, inspiring women, and allowing women to travel with Him, Jesus clearly shows that God doesn't discriminate against gender. He desires an intimate relationship with men and women and wants to use both for His service. In addition, women supported Jesus' ministry with their own provisions and money. These weren't just any women who followed Him. They were women society considered as social outcasts because they had lived in sin, or had unclean conditions of that day.

Jesus extended His everlasting love, compassion and goodness to set these women free from their afflictions. Once healed, they were so deeply grateful, that they whole-heartedly committed their lives to His service. Christ desires the same for us today. He knows that women were created with an innate nurturing ability to passionately love and serve from the depths of our hearts. Once healed and set free, we would become some of His most devoted followers.

With this in mind, our hearts should go out to the many diffi-cult people we encounter today. Like the women who were healed in Jesus' day, He wants to heal all hurting hearts. Many of the diffi-cult people we encounter have been rejected, mistreated, unloved or abused or they feel inadequate within. Or they are deeply dis-appointed with the direction their lives have taken. Even when it's learned behavior, it still originated with someone's shame or pain that affected future generations.

Whether we are right or wrong, good or bad, God loves all peo-ple unconditionally. And He is the only One who can look down the road and see what each person will become in time. Therefore, when "haters" come our way, we should pray for them, forgive them, trust God and do good. You could be the example He uses in their lives to reveal God's presence and greatness. Then trust God to show you how to handle your specific situation. And wheth-er the person changes or not, God gives everyone the opportunity. And remember, while haters are trying to taunt you, someone else is watching you.

In addition, people tend to focus on great positions and ac-complishments on this earth. But the greatest position in the universe is serving as an ambassador of God—His representa-tive on this earth. One day this world and everything in it will all fade away. So God wants to use you right where you are to give others hope and influence someone's eternal destination. That's real greatness.

Therefore, in my conclusion of this whole matter: True suc-cess is when we refuse to tear down what God created for good and yield to His will for our lives. This should be our true aim. Yes, we will face heavy blows of mistreatment, lies, disrespect, insults, criticism and injustice. But these distractions should not push us to despair or knock us out for the final count down. Having faith in God will inspire courage and confidence in our hearts.

Like a woman in labor, we can endure the pain joyfully, when we keep our eyes focused on the prize. You can stand boldly, knowing that God is preparing you for the promise. In God's hands, hardships bring forth something beyond what we could ever imagine, think about, dream of, or hope for. And with the tender hearts God gave women, can you imagine what can happen when women say "yes" to God. We can unite on one accord, with one purpose and with one mind. We could break the hate and help others rise above it. Women fellowships would be like birthing centers to support and encourage one another. Then healing, restoration, wholeness and freedom of individuals, relationships and families would be birthed. Dreams, visions, ministries, businesses and greatness would be birthed. When the floodgates of women's hearts open, God's magnificent treasures can pour in our environments and change the world and lives all around us forever.

So start looking at your challenges from a brand new perspective. Push through the pain and disappointments knowing that you are being shaped to soar to new higher heights. Then when difficult people give you their worst; give *God* the best you've got. And *He* will take what seems impossible to man and make you unstoppable with God. *His* blessings will chase you down and overtake you as you become fit for God to win at life!

Activity #6:

I. *Answer the following questions*

1. How do you feel when your hard work and efforts are not appreciated or recognized?

2. What are some of your motives for doing what you do?

3. What did you learn from your most recent hater's experience?

4. What are some benefits of working hard for God?

5. How do difficult people help your personal and professional growth?

6. How can you change your perspective about the difficult people in your life?

7. What can you do to make peace with the difficult people in your life?

8. How can you prevent the "hater games" from affecting your family and next generation?

9. If your house was a birthing center, what would come forth?

10. How can you give God the best you've got?

II. Change your focus. Write a list of 5-10 unhealthy habits and how you can replace them with heathy behavior. See the examples below.

<u>Old Behavior</u>	<u>New Behavior</u>
1. Criticize others	Encourage others
2. Speak negatively	Speak positively
3. Complain	Make a difference
4. Overeat	Read the Bible, pray, write in journal
5. Snack late at night	Snack on fruits and vegetables
6. Bite nails, smoke	Exercise, walk, stomach crunches
7. Control others	Master your own behavior
8. Want own way	Seek God's ways
9. Overspend	Discover a new hobby, read or write
10. Worry, fear	Meditate on scriptures

Record your old habits and new healthy behavior below:
<u>Old Behavior</u>   <u>New Behavior</u>

III. Answer the following questions. They are only a guide to help you dis-cover your gifts and passion.

   1. What did you love to do as a child?

   2. What are your current hobbies and interests?

   3. What would you study if you could go back to school?

   4. If money was not an option what would you do?

   5. What do you really do well?

6. What people, topics, events or activities capture your attention?

7. What type of people or professionals do you admire?

8. When do you feel the most energized and excited?

9. What do friends and family say make you the most excited?

10. What do friends and family say make them excited about you?

11. What do you do that make a positive difference in the lives of others?

12. When someone does _____, you get upset.

13. When someone does not do _____, you get upset.

14. What type of people or causes pull on your heart strings?

15. If you had the time and resources, where would you volunteer or donate money?

How to increase your income and/or let your passion work for you
The list below serves a dual purpose: It provides options to increase your income until your passion works for you. It can also be used as a guide to make your passion work for you.

Earn more money at your current job: The most obvious way to earn extra money is at your current job. Talk to your manager about working extra hours or overtime. Another option is to pursue a promotion or get prepared for one by exceeding your goals, taking additional training courses or pursuing a degree or more training. In addition, be reliable, on time, consistent and diligent to stand out as an obvious candidate for the next opportunity.

Update your resume and seek a new job. Your current position can give you the experience and skills to apply for a new job. New employers often offer new candidates an increase in salary as an incentive to accept a new position.

Get a part-time job: Working part-time is one of the easiest ways to earn extra money. You can work extra hours in the evenings a few days a week or work on the weekends in your similar field or a different field. A part-time job can help you pay off debt and save sooner. This temporary sacrifice can make a big difference in your bank account and reduce the strain of debt.

Find ways to network. At times, there seem to be more people unemployed than there are available jobs. Applying for jobs online or sending out your resume alone may not be enough to get a job. Ask friends and family members for resources, attend networking organizations and don't limit yourself. The job market has changed and you have to market yourself differently. Who you know can make a big difference. Seeking assistance through an employment or temporary agency can help you get a job quicker or at least get you into the door.

Pursue higher learning: A degree can make you more competitive in the job market and give you a specialty or specific career to pursue to earn more money. Higher learning includes continuing education and training to stay updated with technology and certifications. You can increase your current job skills or seek a new skill to earn more money.

Start your own business: When it comes to starting your own business, the possibilities are unlimited. Your skills, talents and hobbies can be used to increase your income. You can sell arts and crafts, and specialty products. You can offer a variety of services such as designing and making clothes, writing and editing, event planning, coaching, personal training, cosmetology, event planning, photography or cleaning services. You can create web designs, business cards and stationary, or even sell baking goods. The internet makes it easier for many people to start small businesses and on-line stores. Create a website and link to a secure payment site to collect payments for your products and services.

Be a caretaker: You can watch your neighbor's home when they go out of town or take care of their elderly parents, children, or pets. House-sitting, babysitting, or dog walking a few days a week is a rewarding and fun way to put extra money in your wallet, especially if you love children, pets and caring for others.

Sell items you don't use: A garage sell can help you and others by offering furniture, household items and other items you no longer use at a discounted price. Consignment stores are another option to sell clothes, shoes or other items that have been taking up extra space in your closet. You can sell books you no longer use to a used book store and sell your old jewelry to make extra money. You can sell an extra car you no longer drive or need.

Rent out space: If you have extra space in your home you can get a roommate to cut living expenses or rent out a bedroom or part of your house you do not use. Of course, be careful and choose someone you trust. Or you can down-size your home or apartment or consider temporarily staying with relatives to reduce expenses and pay off debt.

Be a motivational speaker: Put your knowledge and skills to use by speaking at workshops, conferences, seminars, retreats or businesses to help others reach their full potential. You do not have to be "the expert" in the topic to share with others. Be knowledgeable and have the passion to inform, convince and inspire. You can share an exciting or fascinating story about your life's experiences. Have such a conviction in your heart that it captivates others to respond and explore what you have learned along the way.

Write a book: Writing a book about your life's experiences, accomplishments, and interests or as a professional in your field is a great way to market yourself. You can plan a book signing, sell your book online and accept engagements to share your passion. There are many affordable self-publishing options available today.

Share the gift of music: The gift of music will be enjoyed forever. You can use your gift of singing or playing instruments for organizations, at weddings and at various events and occasions.

Sell for another company: Direct selling wholesale items for a company can help you earn extra money. Make sure you choose a reputable company and sponsor. Some companies require a start-up cost for the sales kit but avoid companies that require paying a huge membership and fees. And as with anything else in life, the amount of time and energy you invest will determine how much you're able to sell.

Flip houses or apartments: Investing in real estate requires up-front cash, but it can be a great way to earn on your investment. If you are handy with fixing up homes, you can purchase property, renovate, and then resell to earn a huge profit.

When it comes to increasing your income, what's important is to avoid limiting yourself to a traditional "job" or focus solely on starting your own business. Think outside of the box, be creative and find opportunities that fit your availability, lifestyle, talents and skills. Other options are teaching part-time at a college, university or trade school, depending on the educational requirements. Put your skills to use as a consultant or contractor for a company or work for a temp agency. Partner with another business or work on a project for one.

An additional option is to serve as an intern for an organization to get experience for a particular position. Or you can be a personal shopper, a delivery person, a waiter, a tutor or coach, or use your plumbing, painting, gardening and maintenance skills for side jobs. You can provide transportation or cook, sew and do laundry for others. You can teach online courses, work for a company online, take surveys, and buy and sell on the internet. Don't limit yourself to your city and state. There's always the possibility of moving to an area that has more job opportunities in your profession or offers more opportunities to use your gifts, talents, and abilities.

PART TWO:
WINNING INSPIRATIONS

SOMETHING
BEAUTIFUL ABOUT YOU

You were created with special gifts and attributes
To be used in a wonderful way in whatever you do
There's something beautiful about you

The way you give and lend a helping hand
To meet the needs of others whenever you can
There's something beautiful about you

It may be your smile, your laugh, your tender heart
The way you care and make a difference wherever you are
There's something beautiful about you

The way you make people feel or the words you speak
The way you inspire others to be the best they can be
There's something beautiful about you

You have a way that belongs to you alone
No one can take it and make it their own
There's something beautiful about you

You are uniquely made and one of a kind
You are becoming God's masterpiece in His time
There's something beautiful about you

Or maybe you don't realize how special you are
You're a hidden treasure being shaped by God
There's something beautiful about you

Like when diamonds are made deep within the earth
The greater the pressure, the greater their worth
There's something beautiful about you

So don't compare yourself or envy others' gifts and talents
The greatness within you captivates God's heart
There's something beautiful about you

The next time you see an older or younger woman
Tell her to look in heaven's mirror, then boldly say
There's something beautiful about you!

DO YOU
SEE MY SHINE?

People pay attention to women's hair, figure, make-up and
fashion
But with all we've been through, a big question is,
Do they see our shine?

For instance, I've been through more than I ever imagined
I've been hurt and in so much pain
I've cried all night long, but called on Jesus' name
So I ask the question, "Do you see my shine?"

At times, it was too much to bear
I could have thrown in the towel or lost my mind
But today I put my life in *His* hands
Do you see my shine?

People focus on complexion, hair, body parts and sizes
Judging looks is a vicious cycle that conquers and divides
Comparisons lead to jealousy, competition and women dis-
liking one another

Oh women, can't you see, our differences reveal the beauty of God's creativity
Do you see my shine?

I'm a woman who has often been misunderstood
But over these years, heaven's glow has cleansed my heart
I know how to love, forgive and show patience and kindness to others
I now lift women up and embrace all women as heavenly treasures
Do you see *my* shine?

Today I have peace and joy and I'm learning how to trust God in all of my ways
I'm not perfect, but thank God I'm a whole lot better and I am growing day by day
Do you see my shine?

Just like we receive presents to celebrate holidays and special events
And when we rip off the wrapping, the real gift is within
Do you see my shine?

So the next time someone focuses on your looks or compares you to someone else
Remember how far God has brought you and think about what matters most
Then look straight into their eyes, wave to heaven and say
Don't you know I'm wrapped in the beauty of His grace...
Do you see my shine!

INSPIRATION 3

I AM ONE OF A KIND, I AM ME

Like a potter sculpting a masterpiece
God carefully selected my parents' genes
I am one of a kind, I am me

I have my mother's round face and smile
My dad's hairline and almond-shaped eyes
I am one of a kind, I am me

His hazel eyes mixed with her very dark ones
My medium brown eyes reflect the rays of the sun
I am one of a kind, I am me

His family's lighter complexion
Combined with her family's darker skin
Gave me his freckles on a rich caramel blend
I am one of a kind, I am me

My mother's body shape and size
My father's athleticism, strong abs and thighs
I am one of a kind, I am me

I have my mother's short height, but that's alright
A glance in the mirror is my sweet grandma's image
I am one of a kind, I am me

My hair is soft like cotton and gets frizzy and fuzzy
But tells an interesting story of my family's diversity
I am one of a kind, I am me

My dad's joking, laughter and creativity
My mom's compassion and incredible high energy
I am one of a kind, I am me

God combined the characteristics of my mother and father
To create my attributes for my God-given purpose
I am one of kind, I am me

He used incredible wisdom to invest in our design
You too were wonderfully made with a specific purpose in
mind
You are one of a kind, so be you

You don't have to look like or be like someone else
You don't have to compare yourself or envy anyone else
You are one of a kind, so be you

When you embrace the beauty in your creation
You can focus on striving for something greater
You are one of a kind, so be you

Every single attribute is an amazing work of art
Our characteristics reveal a legacy of people chosen by God
When you love yourself, you are free to love someone else
and say...
I am one of a kind, I am me!

A FIT FOR GOD WOMAN

Strengthened in her spirit
Healing in her soul
Caring for her body
Growing stronger in the Lord

She knows who she is
She knows who she belongs to
She holds her head up high, not in arrogance
Her confidence and trust she place in God

She was created to be a queen
A woman of excellence to walk in divine royalty
A woman of integrity, honor and strength
She will not compromise her God-given gifts

Her beauty flows so spiritually deep
It radiates from her countenance for all eyes to see
Chosen as a light to shine in a dark dying world

But first broken, reshaped and designed by God
To reflect His attributes on the earth

A fit for God woman
Who can find her?
Created as a hidden treasure
To be highly valued, cherished and deeply loved

A fit for God woman
Who can find her?
Resting in her heavenly Father's arms
A vessel for *His* love to flow down and touch the earth

A Fit For God Woman!

A FIT FOR GOD WOMAN'S PLEDGE OF HONOR

A *Fit For God Woman's Pledge Of Honor* was created as a guide. Its purpose is to create awareness of unhealthy behavior and habits that tear women down, hinder our love walk and cause divisions in relationships. If you are ready to break the hate and encourage healthy relationships, this pledge is for you. After you read each pledge, check it off. Sign and date at the end to acknowledge that you understand and agree. But remember growth is a process, as we strive to get better day by day. Read each pledge aloud:

1. __I pledge to seek healing and growth in every area of my life to be all that God created me to be.
2. __I pledge to embrace God's love and to love myself to share His incredible love with others.
3. __I pledge to appreciate women's differences and recognize the beauty in God's creativity.
4. __ I pledge to build women up and refuse to tear down what God created as beautiful in His sight.

5. __I pledge to see myself and other women as more than body parts, appearance and possessions; but to celebrate women as special treasures.

6. __I pledge to break down walls of historical trauma and refuse to compare women's complexions, hair, facial features and body shapes, parts and sizes.

7. __I pledge to celebrate other women's gifts and successes, knowing that we all are part of God's greater plan.

8. __I pledge to acknowledge that true success is not based on what I have, but in who I am to reflect God's goodness in the lives of others.

9. __I pledge to build younger women up and to be a role model as the Word of God commands.

10. __I pledge to refuse to compare children's appearances or abilities, to break the vicious cycle of insecurities and not feeling good enough.

11. __I pledge to share with our youth a legacy of God's greatness of creating each of them with a special purpose in mind.

12. __I pledge to refuse to bring negativity and complaining in my environments, but to make a positive difference wherever I go.

13. __I pledge to refuse to cause divisions and conflicts; but to be a peace maker and unite women in God's love.

14. __I pledge to let go of control and to trust God; to focus on mastering my emotions, thoughts, words, and actions to become better.

15. __I pledge to refuse to participate in backbiting, gossiping, lying and two-facedness, which causes divisions, pain and strife.

16. __I pledge to work out disagreements in love; without holding grudges and forgiving others, as my heavenly Father also forgives me.

17. __I pledge to trust God as the Judge and my Defense; and I refuse to retaliate when someone tries to cause me harm.
18. __I pledge to pray for difficult people; who are really the "hurting", who need healing and wholeness from God.
19. __I pledge to pray for the wisdom and strength to deal with difficult people the right way.
20. __I pledge to pray for God's help to become better, to love better and to live a life that brings honor to His wonderful name.

Date:_____

Signature:_____

Printed Name:_____

Congratulations! Your name has been added to A Fit For God Woman's Pledge of Honor's List to break the hate and inspire greatness!

APPENDICES:
MORE WINNING TOPICS

APPENDIX I
WINNING
RELATIONSHIPS ETIQUETTE

1. Treat all people with respect. All human beings were created with a special purpose in mind and deserve to be safe, valued and loved.
2. Be sensitive to other people's emotions and feelings. Everyone was not created the same.
3. Consider how your words, tone, expressions and behavior make others feel. It is not always about you.
4. Think about how gossip, criticizing, and fault-finding hurt you. Why would you want someone else to feel that way? *News Flash*: You are not perfect and have room for growth too.
5. Don't focus on the negative. See the good. There is so much more of God's goodness that surrounds us each and every day.
6. Don't look down on others, unless you are reaching down to pick them up. Every human being was created to be uplifted and encouraged.
7. Know that you were created by *Love* to be loved. And when you love yourself you can genuinely love someone else.
8. Embrace the beauty in your creation to see the beauty in other people's uniqueness.
9. Choose words that bring life. Or if you don't have anything good to say, it is better to say nothing at all. Simply put: build up or shut up.

10. Refuse to gossip and tear others down. If you are bored or idle: get a hobby, exercise, volunteer, read a book, learn a language, mentor a child, or walk for a cause. Use that extra energy to make a positive difference and learn how to replace bad habits with good behavior.

11. Connect to positive purpose-driven people so you can encourage one another to move in the right direction.

12. Confide in someone you can trust, to help you work through your weaknesses and concerns.

13. Look at your friends and the people you connect to. This gives you an idea of your possible weaknesses and opportunities for growth in your life.

14. Notice what you bring to your environments. Do you bring negative energy that creates tension and distress? Or do you bring positive attributes that add value to people's lives?

15. Don't judge a book by its cover. Getting to know someone takes time and patience. If not, you will end up deeply disappointed. Or you can miss a beautiful heart by judging the outside.

16. Take it as a compliment when someone focuses their attention on you. They really admire something about you. And if they copy you, don't get mad. Discover how to use your ability to influence others in a positive way.

17. Seek God to discover the reason for your existence. You won't have time to worry about others when you wholeheartedly focus on God's vision for your life.

18. Do not expect people to think like you, act like you, or be like you. This is a sure sign of limitations and need for growth in your life.

19. Respect people's differences. We have diverse backgrounds, cultures, genetic makeups and experiences that shape our personalities and views.

20. If you find yourself constantly critiquing others or pointing out their flaws, take a good look in the mirror and face what you've been running from.

21. Be yourself. If you have to go along to get along, that is not a genuine relationship. And being yourself is not an excuse to be rude to others by saying, "That's just the way I am".

22. Do not have a conversation when you are angry or frustrated. Let these emotions subside and then speak calmly and respectfully. Hurtful words cannot be taken back.

23. Always be ready to agree to disagree. People will not always see your point of view. We all see life through different colored lenses.

24. Allow people to be themselves. Controlling others can be a form of abuse. It also indicates the need for healing of an underlying issue or it is a sign that you need to learn how to trust God.

25. Strive for success in heaven's eyes. Real success is not measured by income, assets, status, position, education or title. It is based on how you handle God's greatest treasures—His precious people.

26. Ask God to show you how to set boundaries. You may have to love some people from afar or shake the dust off of your feet to stay on the path of becoming healthy and whole.

27. Pray for the wisdom to know how to respond to difficult people in your home, on the job, in church and everywhere you go.

28. Don't get paranoid when you are criticized by others or when they keep a list of your perceived flaws. Relax and trust God with all of your heart. What they do to harm you, God will turn around for your good.

29. Every relationship requires work. And as you grow in a horizontal relationship with God, healthy relationships will naturally follow.

30. Always do good and trust God, even when people don't change or treat you right in return. You will be a winner in God's eyes and *He* will give you a sure reward.

APPENDIX II
BEATING
WORKPLACE BULLYING

We face difficult people on the job every day. But intimidation on the job or "workplace bullying" is often overlooked. It is a serious problem that causes great emotional distress at work. Workplace bullying decreases job morale and productivity and increases job error rates. It increases job absenteeism due to stress-related illnesses. Workplace bullying can cause people to have headaches, digestive problems, body aches and pains, and sleep problems. It can lead to depression and make it difficult to get up in the morning to go to work. It is difficult to function on a daily basis while being made to feel fearful or inadequate or while your performance is scrutinized daily. A supervisor, peer or subordinate can cause employees to experience these feelings. Some signs of workplace bullying include when someone:

- Speaks negatively about one employee to other employees
- Finds fault with an employee's work and only points out mistakes
- Ostracizes an employee and gives him or her the silent treatment
- Yells, shouts or calls an employee out of his or her name
- Sabotages an employee's work performance and reputation
- Makes demeaning and rude remarks about an employee
- Sets an employee up for failure and makes the job difficult
- Blames an employee for mistakes and don't acknowledge his or her short-comings

- Belittles an employee, but takes credit for accomplishments
- Holds an employee accountable for expectations that he or she does not meet
- Does not hold other employees accountable to the same standards
- Keeps an employee out of meetings or do not include him or her in emails
- Avoids speaking to an employee and avoids making eye contact with him or her
- Constantly questions an employee's actions and work performance
- Makes unreasonable demands or overworks an employee
- Acts one way around the employee, but behaves differently around others
- Accuses the employee of being the problem, if the employee confronts the bully

Bullying starts very early in life. School bullies inflict their pain on other children, without understanding their pain within. Surprisingly, adult bullies are common today. Leaders, micromanagers and workplace bullies use their titles and positions to intimidate others. Some overload people with unrealistic goals and expectations as if they are machines, rather than live human beings. They threaten employees' jobs or keep a list to justify a poor performance rating as punishment. Or they are easily agitated or angered, which leads to an explosive temper. Small things cause people who struggle with the inner turmoil of anger to explode.

Workplace bullies don't give others the same respect they desire. They treat others as inferior. They hold others at standards they themselves do not deliver. They are never satisfied because the real anguish is within. Some managers or coworkers exert power over others to gain respect or to avoid becoming a "target". This behavior creates an unhealthy or hostile environment. People tend to walk on eggshells to avoid criticism or confrontation or they feel anxious about their job performance.

Some companies unknowingly created a culture of workplace bullying. This happens when they have allowed it to go on for a long period of time, without taking action. In addition, a highly competitive environment can create this type of culture. In other cases, workplace bullies were awarded or promoted for getting the job done. Upper management failed to recognize that productivity goals were obtained with intimidation tactics. Or they simply didn't care as long as goals were met.

Still, some supervisors show favoritism and allow peers and subordinates to get away with unhealthy habits. Management fail to correct the behavior or don't realize the culture that has been created. Then they unjustly label the target as the problem. Fault-finding also creates an environment of workplace bullying. Whether leaders and senior management accept it or not, bullying is a form of abusive behavior. And this behavior starts at the top. Senior management allows is to happen when they fail to hold the "bully" accountable; or when they expect the "victim" to change to accommodate this behavior.

Every human being has a right to work in a healthy and safe environment. The reality is many companies put profit before people. Or this topic is not a priority. Upper management and HR need to look at the whole picture when an employee is picked out to be criticized or a list is maintained to justify a poor performance. Bullying creates an unhealthy environment where employees cannot function at their best. This makes it very difficult to concentrate and will diminish an employee's overall job performance. Even if the employee is not intimidated or fearful, the distraction alone affects his or her concentration and performance by creating a hostile work environment.

For example, an otherwise outgoing employee may become discouraged, quiet and more withdrawn. Or an employee will have an increase in errors and mistakes and will experience more job absenteeism due to stress. And bullies are so manipulative that they establish a reputation and followers before they attack. Some people are deceived because bullies don't bully everyone. And other people feed their unhealthy emotions and actions. They will go as far to befriend people they once didn't like, just to gain supporters against you. And as with childhood bullies, adults would rather go along to get along too. They find this easier to avoid being considered an outcast or becoming the target. Plus having supporters makes the target look like the real problem.

Absolutely no parent would tolerate their child being bullied in school. Why should the job or other environments where adults congregate be any different? A child bully is more understandable. An adult should have the maturity to respect others, rather than diminish another adult's self-worth and value. But these grown folks express their inner conflicts with temper tantrums by making others feel their turmoil within. They bring their personal issues on the job and expect others to function with their dysfunction.

We spend the majority of our waking hours at work. So I strongly believe that there should be "zero tolerance" or a "No Bully Work Zone". Bullying should be unacceptable behavior. This will benefit both employees and the company. Workplace conduct training with best practices will minimize the consequences of this unhealthy behavior. Not only does workplace bullying has short-term effects, such as decreased performance and high turnover, medical research has indicated that prolonged exposure to stress produces substances in the body that lead to various illnesses and diseases. Over time, experiencing tension for most of the day will deteriorate an employee's overall health and well-being.

Therefore, employees should report bullying immediately to their supervisor or upper management or HR. An employee can first try a one-on-one conversation. But it may not be the best option in some instances, especially if signs of aggression or a pattern of this behavior has been demonstrated. Some employees hesitate or are afraid to speak up for different reasons. But it is important to report it as soon as possible and keep notes of specific incidents (include date, time, action, words and location).

Companies are required to investigate any signs of a hostile work environment and take appropriate actions. If the company fails to protect an employee or fail to correct the behavior, the employee needs to decide what action to take. Options are to apply for another position, leave the company or seek legal counsel. Workplace bullying is a form of harassment and has federal, state and local laws to protect employees. Therefore, legal guidance is an available option as well.

Bullying should not be tolerated anywhere! This abusive behavior should be immediately confronted and dealt with by leaders, management and the company or organization. All people should be held accountable. Once people walk through the doors of the workplace, people should be expected to leave their personal issues behind, show mutual respect to everyone and get the job done. Keep in mind, some people need healing from abusive backgrounds. So disrespectful behavior is their norm. They may need to seek counseling to deal with deeply rooted issues. Or it could be learned behavior that needs to be replaced with best practices for a healthy work environment.

An environment that promotes mutual respect and employee health and success will benefit the company in the long run. Studies show that healthy employees are happier and can better focus on getting the job done. They have increased morale and productivity, reduced job absenteeism, and less stress-related illnesses and medical costs. They have reduced attrition and they create a best place to work.

In addition, those who say they serve Christ and do nothing or contribute to this behavior, may be held accountable to a higher degree. God does not promote His children for personal goals of success, power, popularity or wealth. As we see throughout the Bible, God places His children in positions of influence to make a difference. And as with all strongholds, prayer is desperately needed for guidance to break this vicious cycle. And remember, if God allows you to go through it, He will get you through and then use it. Ultimately, God will use your experiences to build you up to be a blessing to others. And He will show you how to beat the bullying to be free to be all that *He* created you to be!

APPENDIX III
BEST WORKPLACE
PRACTICES

1. Treat all people with respect. Know that there is value and dignity in every position. Imagine what would happen if the cleaning people stopped cleaning your office, garbage cans or restrooms.
2. Respect everyone's differences. No one person knows it all or has it all. It takes a team of people working different skill sets together for overall success.
3. Focus on doing your job and remember why you were hired. Don't worry about people liking you, but they should respect you.
4. Do your best. If you need help, additional skills or knowledge, find the proper resources or training tools to help you succeed.
5. Get a clear understanding of your job description and expectations. It may be in writing or you should have the conversation with your manager or HR for clarity.
6. Take the initiative to have a conversation with your supervisor in advance about your performance. This helps to avoid surprises during evaluation. Plus it gives you time to meet expectations or improve your performance.
7. Don't participate in workplace gossip. It causes division and tension and can create a hostile work environment. Plus remember that a gossiper is most likely talking about you too and can easily turn on you.
8. Don't be a part of the problem, be a part of the solution. Focus on being there to make a difference.

9. Don't judge a person based on someone else's views. People are bias and have expectations of others based on their personality, experiences, background and preferences.

10. If someone disrespects you, attempt to have the conversation with the person. If he or she is not approachable, get the supervisor involved. Escalate to the next level if needed, which may be your HR department.

11. Do not yell, speak rudely or have a conversation when you are angry or frustrated. Wait for the feelings to subside to avoid escalating the situation.

12. Put your personal issues to the side and keep a positive attitude. If you are not a positive person, at least be professional.

13. Do not try to make yourself look better by pointing out people's flaws. If you want to be recognized or promoted, seek additional knowledge and skills for career growth. And have the conversation with your manager for next steps.

14. Know that the best leaders do not tear others down, faultfind and show obvious favoritism. They genuinely desire to help all people succeed and see weaknesses as opportunities for growth.

15. Accept the fact that everyone will not appreciate you. Some people will be jealous or will feel threatened by your personality or talent. So don't be surprised when they find ways to criticize your performance.

16. When faced with workplace difficulties, you have a choice. If you cannot find a solution, decide if you need to find another position or leave the company. Or pray and see if God is trying to sharpen your skills or improve your attitude for a greater opportunity.

17. If you feel that you are experiencing a hostile work environment or discrimination (age, race, gender or religion), go to the proper channels in your company and/or seek legal

guidance. There are local, state and federal laws to protect employees.

18. Maintain your integrity even in an unfair culture or highly competitive environment. Give it the best you've got and always do the right thing.

19. Trust God as your Defense. Refuse to walk around paranoid, suspicious or with a chip on your shoulder. Know that God sees every unfair action and one day everyone will answer to Him.

20. Trust your career and future in God's hands. The Bible is clear that promotions come from God. He has the power to bring one down and uplift another at His appointed time.

APPENDIX IV
CONTROL
THE HEAVY WEIGHT

Like obesity, the heavy weight of "control" is an epidemic in our society today. The word "control" has different meanings. Control is defined as exercising authoritative or dominating influence over; to hold in restraint; to exert power over; to command, master, direct, rule, or regulate; or to repress, restrain, master, and govern. We are controlled or manipulated all of the time. For instance, advertisers tell us what to wear, what to buy, and where to shop. They tell us what's hot and what's not. The mass media tells us how we should think and what should be important to us. They influence our appearance, the careers and jobs we should seek, and who to date or marry.

Then people in our everyday lives seek to stay in control. In the home, on the job, and every place people gather, controllers exert their position, views, and power over others. It is also prevalent in schools as bullies threaten other children to hand over lunch money or personal items. Exerting power seems to be a rush for some people. They feel empowered or superior when they have control over others. Still other individuals find a sense of worth and value by exercising authority over someone else.

Controlling behavior happens for a number of reasons. It generally starts very early in life and is normally determined by upbringing. Seeds of control are planted in the subconscious and like most bad habits are influenced by experiences. Control can develop based on how someone was treated by the authority figure in the home. Or it can happen based on how the authority figure treated the partner or other family members.

It also can happen when there's no authority figure in the home. Then older siblings who care for younger children can develop controlling behavior. To the contrary, younger children can develop controlling behavior because they're used to getting their way. Children also develop control by taking care of themselves at a young age or caring for parents. Or when someone breaks a child's trust, the child grows up and takes control to avoid being hurt, disappointed or abused again.

Parents can also influence children's ability to develop controlling behavior. For instance, explaining how we determine our decisions to children is important. Letting them know that we make our decisions with their best interest in mind teaches them good habits. To the contrary telling them to do what we say because we say so is not showing the love in our decisions. The excuse that we are the parents is not a good reason for our actions. To the contrary, telling children we make our decisions based on our love for them, plants seeds of loving care into their hearts.

As an adult, controlling behavior develops for different reasons. Single parents take control to survive, since he or she was the only person the children could depend on. Then when a partner enters the relationship, it may be difficult to adjust and release the control. Employees can develop controlling behavior when disrespected by peers or managers in the workplace. Once they arrive home they exert power over loved ones. Or the opposite happens. People feel powerless at home and come to work to exert power over others. In other instances, controlling people may be unhappy with their lives and avoid the real problem by taking charge of others.

Controlling behavior is so prevalent, yet it is practically ignored today. Control is often confused with leadership abilities, where people are seen as assertive or proactive, especially in the work force. Then it is often confused with anger. A controlling person may display anger when he or she doesn't get his or her way. Taken further, the need to control leads to manipulation and emotional and verbal abuse. Matter of fact, bullying and domestic violence begins with controlling behavior. With control, there always have to be a winner. And if someone cannot gain control, he or she may escalate to yelling, name-calling, throwing things, intimidation, or rage, until it escalates to physical violence. Or the controller will give his or her partner the silent treatment or threaten to leave the relationship to regain the control.

Controlling others is clearly unhealthy behavior. It goes against God's desire for healthy relationships. And control is a form of emotional and physical bondage. Ephesians 5:21 tells us to submit to one another in the fear of God. Submitting to one another does not mean we become passive and allow others to rule over us in complete authority. Believers choose to mutually submit to one another in love, peace, and harmony as we willingly serve Christ and others. Mutual submission looks out for the best interest of one another. We should be willing to learn from each other for individual and corporate growth. We should embrace each other's differences for healthy relationships.

We all have different perspectives, different ways of doing things and different ideas of how to accomplish specific goals. When someone thinks his or her way is the only way or the best way, this is a sign of control. And healthy relationships in the home set the foundation for strong and healthy relationships on the job, in the church and other environments. On the other hand, unhealthy behavior in the home results in unhealthy behavior every place where people get together. And control is a leader of the pack.

Biblically, the word "control" is combined with the word "self" to form "self-control". In the passages referring to lacking "self-control", the King James Bible describes terms such as "incontinency", "incontinent", and "cannot contain" which basically mean to lack constraint or to lack control. The words "temperance" and "sobriety" used in the KJV refers to self-restraining or self-control (Galatians 5:23; 1 Tim 2:15). According to the Word of God, control is not described in reference to someone else. Control pertains to one's self.

In the eyes of God, the only person you or I should restrain or control is ourselves. We ought to master control or restraint over our thoughts, emotions, words, and actions to reflect a Christ-centered life. If we focus on mastering our own ways, we won't focus on controlling others. "Temperance" or "self-control" is a fruit of the Spirit and is a characteristic of a Spirit-led life. Living a godly life is especially challenging in the world we live in today. When we constantly examine all of our thoughts, motives, words and actions, we won't have time to control someone else. And when we seek healing to be whole in every area of our lives— spiritually, emotionally, socially, financially and physically— it will be impossible to control others.

We all have room for growth. And we will be a work in progress until the day we die. But the reality is people focus on others, to avoid facing their issues within due to denial, bad habits or pain. Ironically, people who tend to control others are always spinning out of control. Every day someone tries to master another person's decisions, behavior and life, while lacking restraint and discipline in their own lives. They struggle with emotional outbursts of anger, temper tantrums, overeating, over shopping and overspending. It can go as far as drug and alcohol use, pre-marital sex with multiple partners, and infidelity in marriage.

The lack of control leads to obesity, illnesses and diseases, financial difficulties, divorce, single-parenting, addictions, stress, depression, and numerous hardships and struggles. It manifests in so many more ways that leads to emotional and physical health consequences. The lack of control has devastating results in our families and communities. Its prevalence in business and the financial arena has resulted in the collapse of the economy, and even criminal activity among those once considered the "elite" in society. This is regardless of race, culture, ethnicity or socioeconomic status.

As human beings, we have natural desires for food, safety, security, companionship, rest, sex and love. Each of these desires is good; but must be used by exercising self-control. If not, our natural desires dominate our lives and dictate our habits and behaviors. Apart from God's will, sin comes when we attempt to fulfill our innate passions. We see this everyday as every possible uncontrollable craving in society has been labeled as an illness, addiction, or disease. Even when one craving is controlled, another one develops to replace the insatiable void within.

God is the only One who can truly fulfill the inner desire that yearns to be loved, safe and secure. Without desiring and receiving the healing power of His love, an inner longing is intensified with every failed attempt. This creates a vicious cycle of defeat that influences generation after generation. In addition, without discovering the reason for our existence, an insatiable hunger remains. Many people continue on a life-long journey attempting to fill this void. When we fail to submit to God's will and His purpose for our lives, our best efforts will not avail.

Connecting to our Creator and seeking Him daily feeds our inner man. In John 4:34 Jesus says, *"My meat is to do the will of Him who sent Me."* Jesus' satisfaction came from pleasing His heavenly Father and doing what God created Him to do. In doing so He found spiritual nourishment and His flesh was under subjection to the Father's will. Connecting to God's vision for His life brought Him great joy and satisfaction within.

There is healing in the Word of God, but we have to open our hearts to receive it. Then we have a choice. We have to be willing to change. When we allow the Word of God to be our instructions for kingdom living and our roadmap for success, we learn that every single day presents opportunities to improve our thoughts, words, actions, choices and decisions. And when you focus on self-control, you can overcome trying to control others. When you place your trust in God, with His help the stronghold of control can be broken.

People who try to control others unknowingly try to take the place of God. He wants us to encourage and guide others. But if you get angry when someone does not take your advice or try to manipulate the situation or person, that's a sure sign of control. And when you give, you should give from the heart, without expecting something in return, or that's a sign of control. Giving can also be a controller's way to maintain control in someone's life. Then when the person no longer goes along with the controller's suggestions, the giving stops or is limited. A genuine giver has no need to announce what they give to others and they don't use giving as a tool to have his or her way with people.

Ultimately, God is the only One who knows the plans and thoughts He has for each of His children's lives. Quite frankly, He doesn't need our help. He chooses to use us for others. God created every human being with a free-will to make his or her own choices. When you try to control or manipulate others, you are doing the opposite of God's will for His creation. Only the enemy of God places people in bondage. And Christ came to set the captives free.

So no matter how you developed the heavy weight of control, when you seek healing, this quality can be used for greater good. God has the divine ingenuity to work all things out for good. A take-charge, task-oriented personality helps you take action for wonderful things to happen. It can be used on the job to help people strive for success, achieve goals and create a best place to work. You can use it to start your own business and pursue the dreams God placed in your heart. In ministry it can help expand God's kingdom throughout the community and the world. You can inspire others to get up from where they are and overcome life's challenges. You can encourage our future generations to live better and strive to be the best they can be. You can help others discover their gifts to fulfill their purpose to the best of their ability.

And when God places you in a position of leadership, He is trusting you with His greatest investment. The best leaders use this quality to develop and bring out the best in people. They embrace differences and see short-comings as opportunities for growth to build people up. God's passion is people. So the best way to defeat control is to let it go and let God use you to make a positive difference in the lives of others. In some instances, you may think you are helping others. But if people feel agitated or oppressed by your actions, or don't feel free to grow into the person God created them to be, it's time to lose the weight of control. Then open your heart and allow God's Spirit to take control of you.

APPENDIX V
SCRIPTURES TO
FOCUS & WIN

God never wants us to harbor ill feelings such as anger, resentment, not forgiving or hatred for anyone. And He never wants us to take matters into our own hands. Even when someone throws harmful blows at you, God still does not want you to retaliate or return hurtful shots. The Word of God is our roadmap and guides us to win at life. It helps control our emotions to deal with life's challenges in a healthy way. God's promises encourage us to hold on until our situation changes or until we change. In time, you will be free from the distractions of a hater's blows, as you place all of your distresses in the hands of God. Then you can focus on becoming all that He created you to be, to do all that He created you to accomplish. As you read the passages, keep in mind that although the word "man" is used in many scriptures, the term addresses mankind (man and woman).

In addition, both the Old and New Testaments Scriptures are included. From the beginning of the Bible until the end, God gives directives on dealing with people who come up against us and other life's challenges. And there are so many Scriptures that pertain to this topic, that it is impossible to list them all. But as you read through this listing, a good practice is to record the ones that touch your heart or pertain to your situation on index cards. Then meditate on them daily to guard your heart and mind. Plus meditating on God's Word will renew your mind and change your life from the inside out. You can also look up additional Scriptures in your Bible concordance. The following are more than enough to you get started to focus and win:

Old Testament Scriptures
Deuteronomy 31:6
Be strong and of good courage, do not fear nor be afraid of them; for the Lord your God, He is the One who goes with you. He will not leave you nor forsake you.

Joshua 1:9
Have I not commanded you? Be strong and of good courage; do not be afraid, nor be dismayed, for the Lord your God is with you wherever you go.

1 Samuel 16:7
But the Lord said to Samuel, Do not look at his appearance or at the height of his stature, because I have refused him. For the Lord does not see as man sees; for man looks at the outward appearance, but the Lord looks at the heart.

1 Samuel 17:47
Then all the assembly shall know that the Lord does not save with sword and spear; for the battle is the Lord's, and He will give you into our hands.

Psalm 1:1-3
Blessed is the man who walks not in the counsel of the ungodly, nor stands in the path of sinners, nor sits in the seat of the scornful; but his delight is in the law of the Lord, and in His law he meditates day and night. He shall be like a tree planted by the rivers of water, that brings forth its fruit in its season, whose leaf also shall nor wither and whatever he does shall prosper.

Psalm 5:12
For You, O Lord will bless the righteous; with favor You will surround him as with a shield.

Psalm 18:6
In my distress I called upon the Lord, and cried out to my God; and He heard my voice from His temple, and my cry came before Him, even to His ears.

Psalm 18:32-33
It is God who arms me with strength, and makes my way perfect. He makes my feet like the feet of deer, and sets me on high places.

Psalm 23:1-3
The Lord is my shepherd, I shall not want. He makes me lie down in green pastures; He leads me beside the still waters. He restores my soul; He leads me in the paths of righteousness for His name's sake.

Psalm 23:5-6
You prepare a table before me in the presence of my enemies; You anoint my head with oil; my cup runs over. Surely goodness and mercy shall follow me all the days of my life; and I will dwell in the house of the Lord forever.

Psalm 27:1
The Lord is my light and my salvation; whom shall I fear? The Lord is the strength of my life; of whom shall I be afraid?

Psalm 34:4
I sought the Lord, and He heard me, and delivered me from all my fears.

Psalm 34:19
Many are the afflictions of the righteous, but the Lord delivers him out of them all.

Psalm 34:18
The Lord is near to those who have a broken heart, and saves such as have a contrite spirit.

Psalm 37:1-4
Do not fret because of evildoers, nor be envious of the workers of iniquity. For they shall soon be cut down like the grass, and wither as the green herb. Trust in the Lord, and do good; dwell in the land, and feed on His faithfulness. Delight yourself also in the Lord, and He shall give you the desires of your heart.

Psalm 37:23-24
The steps of a good man are ordered by the Lord, and he delights in his way. Though he fall, he shall not be utterly cast down; for the Lord upholds him with His hand.

Psalm 37:25
I have been young, and now am old; yet I have never seen the righteous forsaken, nor his descendants begging bread.

Psalm 37:34
Wait on the Lord, and keep His way, and He shall exalt you to inherit the land; when the wicked are cut off, you shall see it.

Psalm 37:39-40
But the salvation of the righteous is from the Lord; He is their strength in the time of trouble, and the Lord shall help them and deliver them; He shall deliver them from the wicked, and save them, because they trust in Him.

Psalm 40:1-3
I waited patiently for the Lord; and He inclined to me, and heard my cry, and also brought me up out of a horrible pit, out of the

miry clay, and set my feet upon a rock, and established my steps. He has put a new song in my mouth—praise God; many will see it and fear, and will trust in the Lord.

Psalm 46:10
Be still, and know that I am God; I will be exalted among the nations, I will be exalted in the earth!

Psalm 75:6-7
For exaltation comes neither from the east nor from the west nor from the south. But God is judge: He puts down one, and exalts another.

Psalm 107:6
Then they cried out to the Lord in their trouble, and he delivered them from all their distresses.

Psalm 107:20
He sent His word and healed them, and delivered from their destructions.

Psalm 110:1
The Lord said to my Lord, "Sit at My right hand, till I make Your enemies Your footstool."

Psalm 118:8-9
It is better to trust in the Lord than to put confidence in man. It is better to trust in the Lord than to put confidence in princes.

Psalm 146:5
Happy is he who has the God of Jacob for his help, whose hope in the Lord his God…

Psalm 146:9
The Lord watches over the stranger; He relieves the fatherless and widow; but the way of the wicked He turns upside down.

Proverbs 3:5-6
Trust in the Lord with all your heart, and lean not on your own understanding; in all your ways acknowledge Him, and He shall direct your paths.

Proverbs 10:12
Hatred stirs up strife. But love covers all sins.

Proverbs 13:20
He who walks with wise men will be wise, but the companion of fools will be destroyed.

Proverbs 15:1-2
A soft answer turns away wrath, but a harsh word stirs up anger. The mouth of the wise uses knowledge rightly, but the mouth of fools pours forth foolishness.

Proverbs 15:3
The eyes of the Lord are in every place, keeping watch on the evil and the good.

Proverbs 16:32
He who is slow to anger is better than the mighty, and he who rules his spirit than he who takes a city.

Proverb 20:22
Do not say, "I will recompense evil"; wait on the Lord, and He will save you.

Proverbs 22:24-25
Make no friends with an angry man, and with a furious man do not go, lest you learn his ways and set a snare for your soul.

Proverbs 24:16
A righteous man may fall seven times and rise again, but the wicked shall fall by calamity.

Proverbs 24:17-18
Do not rejoice when your enemy falls, and do not let your heart be glad when he stumbles; lest the Lord see it, and it displease Him, and He turn away His wrath from Him.

Proverbs 25:21-22
If your enemy is hungry, give him bread to eat; and if he is thirsty, give him water to drink; for so you will heap coals of fire on his head, and the Lord will reward you.

Proverbs 26:27
Whoever digs a pit will fall into it, and he who rolls a stone will have it roll back on him.

Proverbs 29:11
A fool vents all his feelings, but a wise man holds them back.

Isaiah 26:3-4
You will keep him in perfect peace, whose mind is stayed on you, because He trusts in You. Trust in the Lord forever, for in YAH, the Lord, is everlasting strength.

Isaiah 40:28-29
Have you not known? Have you not heard? The everlasting God, the Lord, the Creator of the ends of the earth, neither faints nor

is weary. His understanding is unsearchable. He gives power to the weak, and to those who have no might He increases strength.

Isaiah 40:30-31
Even the youths shall faint and be weary, and the young men shall utterly fall, but those who wait on the Lord shall renew their strength; they shall mount up with wings as eagles, they shall run and not be weary, they shall walk and not faint.

Isaiah 41:10
Fear not, for I am with you; be not dismayed, for I am your God. I will strengthen you, yes, I will help you, I will uphold you with My righteous right hand.

Isaiah 43:10
You are my witnesses, says the Lord, and My servant whom I have chosen, that you may know and believe Me, and understand that I am He. Before Me, there was no God formed, nor shall there be after Me.

Isaiah 43:18-19
Do not remember the former things, nor consider the things of old. Behold, I will do a new thing, now it shall spring forth; shall you not know it? I will even make a road in the wilderness and rivers in the desert.

Isaiah 61:7
Instead of your shame you shall have double honor, and instead of confusion they shall rejoice in their portion. Therefore in their land they shall possess double; everlasting joy shall be theirs.

Isaiah 54:4
Do not fear, for you will not be ashamed; nor be disgraced, for you will not be put to shame; for you will forget the shame of your youth, and will not remember the reproach of your widowhood anymore.

Isaiah 54:17
No weapon formed against you shall prosper, and every tongue which rises against you in judgment you shall condemn.

Isaiah 59:19
So shall they fear the name of the Lord from the west, and His glory from the rising of the sun; when the enemy comes in like a flood, the Spirit of the Lord will lift up a standard against him.

Jeremiah 29:11
For I know the thoughts that I think toward you, says the Lord, thoughts of peace and not of evil, to give you a future and a hope.

Jeremiah 33:3
Call to Me, and I will answer you, and show you great and mighty things, which you do not know.

Habakkuk 2:2-3
Then the Lord answered me and said: Write the vision and make it plain on tablets, that he may run who reads it. For the vision is yet for an appointed time; but at the end it will speak, and it will not lie. Though it tarries, wait for it; because it will surely come, it will not tarry.

Habakkuk 2:4
Behold the proud, his soul is not upright in him; but the just shall live by his faith.

New Testament Scriptures
Matthew 5:9-10
Blessed are the peacemakers, for they shall be called sons of God. Blessed are those who are persecuted for righteousness sake; for theirs is the kingdom of heaven.

Matthew 5:11-12
Blessed are you when they revile and persecute you, and say all kinds of evil against you falsely for My sake. Rejoice and be exceedingly glad, for great is your reward in heaven...

Matthew 5:16
Let your light shine before men, that they may see your good works and glorify your Father in heaven.

Matthew 5:44-45
But I say to you, love your enemies, bless those who curse you, do good to those who hate you, and pray for those who spitefully use you and persecute you....

Matthew 7:3-4
But why do you look in the speck in your brother's eye, but do not consider the plank in your own eye? Or how can you say to your brother, 'Let me remove the speck out of your eye'; and look, a plank is in your own eye? Hypocrite! First remove the plank from your own eye, and then you will see clearly to remove the speck out of your brother's eyes.

Matthew 11:28-30
Come to Me, all you who labor and are heavy laden, and I will give you rest. Take My yoke upon you and learn from Me, for I am gentle and lowly in heart, and you will find rest for your souls. For My yoke is easy and My burden is light.

Mathew 18:15
Moreover if your brother sins against you, go tell him his fault between you and him alone. If he hears you, you have gained your brother.

Matthew 20:16
So the last will be first, and the first will be last. For many are called, but few chosen.

Mark 11:22-24
So Jesus answered them and said to them, "Have faith in God. For assuredly, I say to you, whoever says to this mountain, 'Be removed and be cast into the sea, and does not doubt in his heart, but believes that those things he says will come to pass, he will have whatever he says, "Therefore I say to you, whatever things you ask when you pray, believe that you receive them, and you will have them.

Mark 11:25-26
And whenever you stand praying, if you have anything against anyone, forgive him, that your Father in heaven may also forgive your trespasses. But if you do not forgive, neither will your Father in heaven forgive your trespasses.

Luke 6:27-28
But I say to you who hear: Love your enemies, do good to those who hate you, bless those who curse you, and pray for those who spitefully use you.

Luke 6:32
But if you love those who love you what credit is that to you? For even sinners love those who love them.

Luke 6:45
A good man out of the good treasure of his heart brings forth good, and an evil man out of the evil treasure of his heart brings forth evil. For out of the abundance of the heart his mouth speaks.

Luke 10:19-20
Behold, I give you authority to trample on serpents and scorpions, and over all the power of the enemy, and nothing shall by any means harm you. Nevertheless do not rejoice in this, that the spirits are subject to you, but rather rejoice because your names are written in heaven.

Luke 18:27
But He said, "The things which are impossible with men are possible with God."

John 10:10
The thief does not come except to steal and to kill, and to destroy. I have come that they may life, and that they may have it more abundantly.

John 15:12
This is my commandment, that you love one another as I have loved you.

John 15:18-19
If the world hates you, you know that it hated Me before it hated you. If you were of the world, the world would love its own. Yet because I chose you out of the world, therefore the world hates you.

John 16:33
These things I have spoken to you, that in Me you may have peace. In the world you will have tribulation; but be of good cheer, I have overcome the world.

1 Corinthians 10:13
No temptation has overtaken you except such as is common to man; but God is faithful, who will not allow you to be tempted

beyond what you are able, but with the temptation will also make the way of escape, that you may be able to bear it.

1 Corinthians 9:25-26
Therefore I run thus: not with uncertainty. Thus I fight: not as one who beats the air. But I discipline my body and bring it into subjection, lest, when I have preached to others, I myself should become disqualified.

1 Corinthians 5:33
Do not be deceived: "Evil company corrupts good habits."

1 Corinthians 15:57
But thanks be to God, who gives us the victory through our Lord Jesus Christ.

1 Corinthians 15:58
Therefore, my beloved brethren, be steadfast, immovable, always abounding in the work of the Lord, knowing that your labor is not in vain in the Lord.

2 Corinthians 1:3-4
Blessed be the God and Father of our Lord Jesus Christ, the Father of mercies and God of all comfort, who comforts us in all our tribulation, that we may be able to comfort those who are in any trouble, with the comfort with which we ourselves are comforted by God.

2 Corinthians 4:7
But we have this treasure in earthen vessels, that the excellence of the power may be of God and not of us.

2 Corinthians 4:8-9
We are hard pressed on every side, yet not crushed, we are perplexed, but not in despair, persecuted, but not forsaken; struck down, but not destroyed...

2 Corinthians 5:17
Therefore, if anyone is in Christ, he is a new creation; old things have passed away; behold, all things have become new.

2 Corinthians 10:4-5
For the weapons of our warfare are not carnal but mighty in God for pulling down strongholds, casting down every high thing that exalts itself against the knowledge of God, bringing every thought into captivity to the obedience of Christ.

2 Corinthians 12:9
And He said to me, "My grace is sufficient for you, for My strength is made perfect in weakness."

2 Corinthians 13:11
Finally, brethren, farewell. Become complete. Be of good comfort, be of one mind, live in peace; and the God of love and peace will be with you.

Romans 5:5
Now hope does not disappoint, because the love of God has been poured out in our hearts by the Holy Spirit who was given to us.

Romans 8:28
And we know all things work together for good to those who love God, to those who are the called according to His purpose.

Romans 8:31

What then shall we say to these things? If God is for us, who can be against us?

Romans 8:37

Yet in all these things we are more than conquerors through Him who loved us.

Romans 8:38

For I am persuaded that neither death nor life, nor angels nor principalities nor powers, nor things present nor things to come, nor height nor depth, nor any other created thing, shall be able to separate us from the love of God which is in Christ Jesus our Lord.

Romans 12:1-2

I beseech you therefore, brethren, by the mercies of God, that you present your bodies a living sacrifice, holy, acceptable to God, which is your reasonable service. And do not be conformed to this world, but be transformed by the renewing of your mind, that you may prove what is that good and acceptable and perfect will of God.

Romans 12:17-21

Repay no one evil for evil. Have regard for good things in the sight of all men. If it is possible, as much as depends on you, live peaceably with all men. Beloved, do not avenge yourselves, but rather give place to wrath; for it is written, "Vengeance is Mine, I will repay," says the Lord. Therefore if your enemy hungers, feed him; if he thirsts, give him a drink; for in so doing you will heap coals of fire on his head. Do not be overcome by evil, but overcome evil with good.

Romans 13:4-8
Love suffers long and is kind; love does not envy, love does not parade itself, is not puffed up; does not behave rudely, does not seek its own; is not provoked, thinks no evil; does not rejoice in iniquity, but rejoices in the truth; bears all things, believes all things, hopes all things, endures all things. Love never fails.

Romans 16:17
Now I urge you, brethren, note those who cause divisions and offenses, contrary to the doctrine which you have learned, and avoid them.

Galatians 1:10
For do I now persuade men, or God? Or do I seek to please men? For if I still pleased men, I would not be a servant of Christ.

Galatians 5:1
Stand fast therefore in the liberty by which Christ has made us free, and do not be entangled again with a yoke of bondage.

Galatians 5:22-23
But the fruit of the Spirit is love, joy, peace, longsuffering, kindness, goodness, faithfulness, gentleness, self-control....

Galatians 6:1
Brethren, if a man is overtaken in any trespass, you who are spiritual restore such a one in a spirit of gentleness, considering yourself, lest you also be tempted.

Galatians 6:7
Do not be deceived, God is not mocked; for whatever a man sows, that he will also reap.

Galatians 6:9
And let us not grow weary while doing good, for in due season we shall reap if we do not lose heart.

Ephesians 1:2
Blessed be the God and Father of our Lord Jesus Christ, who has blessed us with every spiritual blessing in the heavenly places in Christ...

Ephesians 4:26
Be angry, and do not sin; do not let the sun go down on your wrath, nor give place to the devil.

Ephesians 4:29
Let no corrupt communication proceed out of your mouth, but what is good for necessary edification, that it may impart grace to the hearers.

Ephesians 4:31-32
Let all bitterness, wrath, anger, clamor, and evil speaking be put away from you, with all malice. And be kind to one another, tenderhearted, forgiving one another, just as God in Christ also forgave you.

Ephesians 5:1-2
Therefore be followers of God as dear children. And walk in love, as Christ also has loved us and given Himself for us, an offering and a sacrifice to God for a sweet smelling aroma.

Ephesians 5:8
For you were once darkness, but now you are light in the Lord. Walk as children of light.

Ephesian 6:10
Finally brethren, be strong in the Lord and in the power of His might.

Ephesians 6:11
Put on the whole armor of God, that you may be able to stand against the wiles of the devil.

Philippians 2:3-4
Let nothing be done through selfish ambition or conceit, but in lowliness of mind let each esteem others better than himself. Let each of you look out not only for his own interests, but also for the interests of others.

Philippians 3:13-14
Brethren, I do not count myself to have apprehended; but one thing I do, forgetting those things which are behind and reaching forward to those things which are ahead. I press toward the goal for the prize of the upward call of God.

Philippians 4:6-7
Be anxious for nothing, but in everything by prayer and supplication, with thanksgiving, let your requests me made known to God; and the peace of God, which surpasses all understanding, will guard your hearts and minds through Christ Jesus.

Philippians 4:8
Finally, brethren, whatever things are true, whatever things are noble, whatever things are just, whatever things are pure, whatever things are lovely, whatever things are of good report, if there is any virtue and if there is anything praiseworthy—medicate on these things.

Philippians 4:13
I can do all things through Christ who strengthens me.

Philippians 4:19
And my God shall supply all your need according to His riches in glory by Christ Jesus.

Colossians 3:23-24
And whatever you do, do it heartily, as to the Lord and not to men, knowing that from the Lord you will receive the reward of the inheritance, for you serve the Lord Jesus.

Colossians 3:25
But he who does wrong will be repaid for the wrong he had done, and there is no partiality.

2 Timothy 1:7
For God has not given us a spirit of fear, but of power and of love and of a sound mind.

Hebrews 11:1
Now faith is the substance of things hoped for, the evidence of things not seen.

Hebrews 11:6
But without faith it is impossible to please God, for he who comes to God must believe that He is, and that He is a rewarder of those who diligently seek Him.

Hebrews 12:1-2
Therefore we also, since we are surrounded by so great a cloud of witnesses, let us lay aside every weight, and the sin which so easily

ensnares us, and let us run with endurance the race that is set before us, looking unto Jesus, the author and finisher of our faith, who for the joy that was set before Him endured the cross, despising the shame, and has sat down at the right hand of the throne of God.

James 1:2-4
My brethren, count it all joy, when you fall into various trials, knowing that the testing of your faith produces patience. But let patience have its perfect work, that you may be complete, lacking nothing.

James 1:5
If any of you lacks wisdom, let him ask of God, who gives to all liberally and without reproach, and it will be given to him.

James 1:19
Therefore, my beloved brethren, let every man be swift to hear, slow to speak, slow to wrath; for the wrath of man does not produce the righteousness of God.

James 3:8-10
But no man can tame the tongue. It is an unruly evil, full of deadly poison. With it we bless our God and Father, and with it we curse men, who have been made in the similitude of God. Out of the same mouth proceed blessing and cursing. My brethren, these things ought not be so.

James 4:6-8
But He gives more grace. Therefore He says: "God resists the proud, but gives grace to the humble." Therefore submit yourselves to God. Resist the devil and he will flee from you. Draw near to God and He will draw near to you...

James 4:10
Humble yourself in the sight of the Lord, and He will lift you up.

James 4:17
To him who knows to do good and does not do it, to him it is sin.

James 5:9
Do not grumble against one another, brethren, lest you be condemned. Behold the Judge is standing at the door!

1 Peter 5:5
Likewise, you younger people, submit yourselves to your elders. Yes, all of you be submissive to one another, and be clothed with humility, for "God resists the proud, but gives grace to the humble."

1 Peter 5:6
Therefore humble yourselves under the mighty hand of God, that He may exalt you in due time, casting all your care on Him, for He cares for you.

1 Peter 5:10
But may the God of all grace, who called us to His eternal glory by Christ Jesus, after you have suffered a while, perfect, establish, strengthen and settle you.

1 John 1:9
If we confess our sins, He is faithful and just to forgive us our sins and to cleanse us from all unrighteousness.

1 John 4:20
If someone says, "I love God," and hates his brother, he is a liar; for he who does not love his brother whom he has seen, how can he love God whom he has not seen?

1 John 4:7-8
Beloved, let us love one another for love is of God; and everyone who loves is born of God and knows God. He who does not love does not know God, for God is love.

Jude v. 24-25
Now to Him who is able to keep you from stumbling, and to present you faultless before the presence of His glory with exceeding joy, to God our Savior, who alone is wise, be glory and majesty, dominion and power, both now and forever. Amen.

AN INSPIRATIONAL BOOK

Dogs Gotta Be In Heaven: A Loving Memory of A Companion & Friend.
If you have a dog, have ever lost one or you are considering getting
a pet, this book is a *must* read. As an animal lover since childhood,
La Vita Weaver captures the love and devotion felt between pets
and their human families. This touching message weaves together
life lessons on love, happiness, purpose and passion. It reveals how
our cherished companions are amazing blessings on earth. Can
you believe they were created for a greater purpose?

ABOUT THE AUTHOR

La Vita Weaver is an inspirational speaker, *author*, fitness trainer and CPR instructor. As a mother of three, she knows first-hand how struggling with extra weight affects every area of one's life. Her inspirational story of overcoming bingeing and depression is shared in her faith-based health and fitness book *Fit For God: The 8-Week Plan That Kicks the Devil OUT and Invites Health and Healing IN.*

La Vita is an ordained evangelist and has taught faith and fitness for over twenty five years. She shared the joy of fitness internationally as cohost of Trinity Broadcasting Network's (TBN's) popular fitness show "TotaLee Fit", with 8-Times Mr. Olympia. She produced and hosted "Eternally Fit", an award-winning local cable health and fitness show. She also originated Hallelujah! Aerobics For Body and Spirit, the first Christian exercise program of its kind.

Her success story aired on the popular *TBN* show "Praise the Lord" and the well-known "700 Club". Articles appeared in *Essence, Excellence, Heart & Soul,* and *Shape* magazines and other publications. In addition, she has served in women's ministry for over twenty five years, empowering women of all walks of life to live victoriously. Plus for the past decade, she has worked as a financial specialist, teaching the youth and adults financial fitness.

La Vita's interdisciplinary expertise fuels her passion as a "fit for God trainer" to inspire the whole person. She deeply desires for all people to live a better quality of life, inside and out. Her dynamic messages uplift the most downtrodden souls and her genuine enthusiasm and joy for life is contagious!

To schedule a speaking engagement or a Fit For God Workshop or for more information, contact:

Fit For God Ministries:
(844) Fit-4God
(844) 348-4463
(703) 763-7678

info@fitforgod.com
www.FitForGod.com